STRANGE But True
Baseball Stories

STRANGE
But True
Baseball Stories

by Furman Bisher

ILLUSTRATED WITH
PHOTOGRAPHS

RANDOM HOUSE · NEW YORK

This title was originally catalogued by the Library of Congress as follows:

Bisher, Furman.
    Strange but true baseball stories. New York, Random House ₁1966₁

    186 p. ports. 24 cm. (Little League library, 4)

1. Baseball stories—Juvenile literature. ɪ. Title.

GV873.B5   796.3570922   65–10492

Library of Congress   ₁8₁

Photograph Credits: Odell Barbary, page 32; Furman Bisher, pages 45, 88; Culver Pictures, pages 79, 92, 127, 128, 149, 160; The *News*, page 182; Sy Seidman, page 162; United Press International, pages 10, 12, 60, 72, 74, 104, 108, 116, 137, 141, 143, 169; Wide World, pages 4, 7, 20, 36, 40, 53, 55, 62, 67, 80, 100, 113, 119, 135, 146, 166, 181.

Cover art by Tom Beecham

Manufactured in the United States of America

Designed by Jackie Corner

Trade Ed.: ISBN: 0-394-80184-9   Lib. Ed.: ISBN: 0-394-90184-3

CONTENTS

INTRODUCTION

There is a popular misconception that baseball is a game played nine men to the side. This is for narrow people, those who believe that horseshoes can be played only by horses.

Baseball can be played by any number from two on up. It can be played late at night, early in the morning, in the middle of the afternoon, even in the dead of winter, around a pot-bellied stove. As long as two people get together who like to tell stories, baseball can be played anywhere.

Usually, the baseball story teller has a slight inclination to exaggerate. There is something exciting about a baseball story laced with the embellishment of 20 years or more even if it sometimes departs from the boundaries of truth.

The stories in this book are different. Some are strange, some are uncommon, some are almost unbelievable. Some are old, some have never been told before. Not all of the people in this book are famous. Some are like actors who have only one short line in a drama, then disappear and never appear again. These stories have only one thing in common: they actually did happen.

Getting these stories together required the help of other people. Those whose personal assistance or written material contributed most were Lowell Reidenbaugh of the *Sporting News,* Phil Howser of the Charlotte (N. C.) baseball club; Lee Allen of the Baseball Hall of Fame, Harold Kaese of Boston, Charles Einstein of San Francisco, Herbert Simon of *Baseball Digest* and Al Silverman of *Sport* Magazine. To all of them, and others who responded with willingness, I am grateful.

And if I have helped the reader learn to enjoy the "hot stove" game, then my purpose has been achieved.

Furman Bisher
Sports Editor
Atlanta *Journal*

1
Immortal by Accident

By the time he was nineteen years old, Stan Musial was playing his third season of professional baseball as a pitcher for the Daytona Beach Islanders in Florida. Although Daytona Beach did not play the best kind of baseball, Stan was happy doing the thing he loved—pitching. During his first two seasons in the minors Stan's wildness had held him back. At Daytona Beach, though, he had apparently found his control. By early August he had won seventeen games.

Then dawned what seemed to be the darkest day of Musial's life. His manager, Dickie Kerr, had discovered that Musial was also an effective hitter, and used him in the outfield many times when he wasn't pitching. On August 11, 1940, Musial was playing center field for the Islanders. He had pitched the night before.

With two out, a batter hit a sinking line drive in Musial's direction, and he made a run for the ball. He had often made shoetop catches, then hit the ground doing an intentional somersault. He wasn't showing off; Musial felt that it was the best way to protect his catch.

He made the catch on the run and turned his usual somersault. But somehow he miscalculated. As he hit the ground, he felt an awful pain in his pitching shoulder. He held on to the ball for the third out,

3

Musial broke into baseball in 1938 as a pitcher with Williamston, Pennsylvania.

but as he ran for the dugout he was clutching his shoulder. Dickie Kerr intercepted him near the third-base coaching box and asked if anything was wrong. Musial said it was only a slight pain that would soon go away. But it didn't. The shoulder ached all night as Stan fought to get to sleep. The next day Musial refused to tell Kerr that he was still in pain.

His turn to pitch came up two days later, and he accepted his assignment without a murmur. The opponent was Sanford, a strong team. The shoulder ached as he warmed up, and it ached as he pitched. He beat Sanford 5–4, but it was his last victory of the season.

Musial started again a few days later against Orlando. There was no escaping the terrible pain this time. It was more than he could bear. The Orlando team hit him hard, and he had to leave the game early.

Here he was, a young pitcher from steel-mill country, with a wife expecting a baby—and he himself had a bad arm. The situation looked hopeless to Musial. "Don't you think I ought to go home and find a job in the mills and forget baseball?" Musial asked Kerr the next morning.

"Not yet, Stan," Kerr told his young player. He had developed a fondness for the boy; he admired his good habits and his willingness as a player. Kerr had been a pitcher on the infamous Chicago Black Sox of 1919, the American League champions who sold out to gamblers in the World Series, agreeing to lose to the Cincinnati Reds. Kerr was one of the players who remained loyal to his team. He had won two games from Cincinnati. As a result, he had particular respect for a young man with character as well as talent.

Kerr told Musial that he was a good enough hitter to succeed even if his pitching arm didn't improve. To help the young player, Kerr invited Musial and his wife to live with him until their baby was born.

The Musials moved in with the Kerrs. When the

baby was born, the grateful young couple named him Richard Kerr Musial. Although the pain soon disappeared in Musial's shoulder, full strength never did return. But by the end of the season, he was able to throw well enough to play in the outfield again.

The Daytona Beach team was a farm club of the St. Louis Cardinals. When Musial's batting average rose to .311, he was invited to the Cardinals' biggest minor league camp the next spring. He reported as a pitcher and worked with the pitchers until it became apparent that he could no longer compete because of his bad arm.

One day the head of the Cardinal organization, Branch Rickey, one of the most respected judges of baseball talent, came out to watch the farm clubs play. Musial was in the outfield although he still registered on the camp roster as a pitcher.

After watching him only once at bat, Rickey exclaimed: "That man's not a pitcher! He's a hitter!"

Mr. Rickey soon learned that Dickie Kerr had already discovered Musial's hitting talent. Before the season ended, Musial was playing for the Cardinals. He moved rapidly through the minors from Daytona Beach to Springfield, Missouri, to Rochester, New York, and finally to St. Louis. He batted .379 at Springfield and .326 at Rochester. During the last weeks of the season he batted an amazing .426 for

Musial demonstrates the form that made him one of the sport's greatest hitters.

the Cardinals.

Musial retired after the 1963 season. He had led the National League in batting seven times, made 3,630 hits and 475 home runs, driven home 1,951 runs, and averaged .331 over a 22-season career.

Some of baseball's most exciting discoveries have been made by accident. Had it not been for that tumble he took on the night of August 11, 1940, one of the sport's greatest hitters might never have been found.

2
The Greatest Defeat

When Harvey Haddix of the Pittsburgh Pirates went out to warm up for the game against Milwaukee on the night of May 29, 1959, he felt sluggish. His fast ball didn't have its usual zing and his curve ball wasn't snapping the way a Haddix curve was supposed to snap.

He had been fighting a cold and had spent most of the day on the plane to Milwaukee. He wasn't exactly tired, but he was low on vitality.

"I don't feel sharp," he told his manager when he returned to the dugout. "I'll just have to do the best I can as long as I can."

At the end of nine innings, Haddix had not allowed a single Brave to reach first base: he had pitched a perfect regulation game. But the Pirates, although they had put men on base several times, had not been able to score against the Brave's pitcher Lew Burdette. So the game went into extra innings.

In the top of the tenth inning, the Pirates threatened. With one man on and one out, Dick Stuart, a dangerous slugger, came up as a pinch hitter. When he met one of Burdette's pitches, it looked and sounded like a home run. But the center fielder backed up against the fence and pulled it in. The next batter went out, too. The Pirates had failed again to give Haddix the one run he needed for victory.

Haddix kept his perfect game alive through the

9

The determined Haddix kept his perfect game alive through the tenth, eleventh and twelfth innings.

tenth, eleventh and twelfth innings. Thirty-six Braves had come to bat and gone out in order. The Braves' line-up was one of the most dangerous in the majors, including such sluggers as Hank Aaron, Ed Mathews, Joe Adcock and Del Crandall. Yet no one had received as much as a walk.

But the Pirates, who were much more successful at hitting the ball, were no more successful than the Braves in scoring. At the end of the Pirates' half of the thirteenth inning, there was still no score.

When Haddix came out to pitch in the bottom of

the thirteenth, Felix Mantilla, the Braves' second baseman was the first batter. He hit a sharp grounder to
the Pirates' third baseman, Don Hoak. In his hurried
effort to keep Haddix' perfect game alive, Hoak threw
low to first and Mantilla was safe on his error. The
next batter, Ed Mathews, sacrificed Mantilla to second.

Now the perfect game was gone and Haddix gave
Hank Aaron an intentional walk so that the Pirates
would have a chance for a double play. This brought
up Joe Adcock with men on first and second.

Although Adcock had struck out twice and
grounded out twice, he was one of the most dangerous hitters in the league. On the second pitch, he
swung and drove a fly into deep right-centerfield.
Center fielder Bill Virdon backed up all the way to
the wall, but the ball sailed just over his glove and
into the stands.

Now, Haddix' perfect game ended as a farce. Mantilla rounded third and came in with the winning run,
but Aaron, who thought that the ball was still inside
the park and that the game had ended when Mantilla
touched home, rounded second and then headed for
the dugout. Adcock continued on around the bases,
running out his home run.

The Braves, recognizing Aaron's mistake, rushed
him back out on the field where he touched second
base again and then completed his circuit of the bases.

Adcock followed him, touching each base behind him. But it was too late. The umpires ruled Adcock out for passing Aaron on the bases. Adcock's home run was changed to a double in the record books, although Aaron's run was allowed to score.

But the game had ended for Haddix when the first run scored. In three hours and nearly thirteen complete innings, he had struck out eight men, walked only one intentionally and allowed only one hit. His only mistake was one pitch to Joe Adcock.

"I knew I had a no-hitter," he said later in the clubhouse. "I could tell by the scoreboard. But the game had gone so long that I'd lost track of the innings and I wasn't sure if anybody had been on base or not."

Everyone left the park that night thinking the Braves had won 2–0 and it wasn't until the next morning that the official score was recorded. Warren Giles, president of the National League, ruled that the Braves had won by only one run. Since Adcock's hit had been scored a double, he said, it was not logical to count Aaron's run. Only Mantilla had legally scored and the score books were amended to read: Braves 1, Pirates 0.

But the change of score was little consolation for Haddix. He had pitched a magnificent game and yet had gone down in defeat.

fter the disaster in the thirteenth inning, Haddix is consoled by 'ittsburgh manager Danny Murtaugh.

3

The One-Armed Big Leaguer

Peter Wyshner was fascinated by trains. He would stand by the tracks near his house in Nanticoke, Pennsylvania, and watch the big engines tug their cargoes of freight and coal to distant places.

One day he had an urge to ride on one of the trains. When you're six years old, he thought, it's time to see some of the world. Soon a freight train came along on its way from Wilkes-Barre, seven miles away. It was moving slowly but it seemed fast to a six-year-old. As little Peter reached for the brakeman's ladder, his hand slipped and he fell into the path of the train. That night at the hospital, doctors decided to amputate the boy's right arm because it was so badly damaged.

From then on, Peter had to learn to live with only one arm. He had been naturally right-handed, and so he had to learn to write, eat and brush his teeth with his left hand.

When Pete began playing baseball, he discovered it was difficult to play with only one arm. How do you catch the ball and then throw it? How do you swing a bat and hit the ball? And how do you run? Few people realize that a runner's arms are important because they help him keep his balance.

Despite the difficulties, Peter played baseball whenever he got the chance. When he was ten years old, one of the sandlot teams in Nanticoke let him be the

15

batboy. He got to watch good players almost every day and he learned much about the game. But he had to learn for himself how to overcome his handicap.

Then something happened that made Peter determined to become a good baseball player. Playing a "pickup" game one day, he slid hard into the catcher, a big, burly boy. The slide was so forceful that the ball was knocked out of the catcher's mitt.

The angry catcher got up snarling. "Why, if you had two arms I'd smash your nose," he said.

Peter became angry, too, and soon forced the catcher to take back his insult. He resolved to show the catcher and everyone else that he could outshine them all.

When he was old enough, he began playing for money on semiprofessional teams around Nanticoke. Players on semiprofessional teams work at a regular job during the week and play for the company team on evenings and weekends. He even changed his last name to Gray so that people could spell and remember it more easily. One Sunday he presented himself to Max Rosner, the man who operated the Bushwicks of Brooklyn, New York, one of the most famous semiprofessional teams in America.

"I can help your team, Mr. Rosner," Pete told him.

Max Rosner took one look at the one-armed man

and snapped back: "Is this your way of crashing the gate?"

Pete reached into his pocket and pulled out a ten-dollar bill. He didn't have much money, but he was willing to stake it on his ability.

"Take this," Pete said, "and if I don't make good, keep it."

Pete Gray eventually got his ten dollars back and became the Bushwicks' greatest drawing card. News of the one-armed player spread and people flocked to Dexter Park in Brooklyn to see Pete Gray. This pleased Pete, but he had even bigger ambitions. He wanted to play in the majors. And he knew that he would have to play for a professional team before the major leagues would even notice him.

Finally, in 1942, Mickey O'Neill, who managed a professional team at Three Rivers, Quebec, part of the Canadian-American League, said he would give Pete Gray a chance. O'Neill never regretted his decision. Pete batted .381 at Three Rivers, and if he hadn't broken his collarbone during the season, he would have qualified to lead the league.

Pete had learned to make catches in the outfield, and throw the ball to the infield. His movement was so swift that it could hardly be followed by the naked eye. He would catch the ball in a small, padless glove. Then he would flip the ball in the air while deftly removing the glove by sticking it under the stub of a right arm. As the ball came down, he caught it and made his throw.

Professional baseball in the United States was learning about Pete Gray's talents, too. In 1943, he played for the Memphis Chicks, members of the Southern Association, one of the toughest minor leagues.

His start was slow, and there were times when Memphis Manager Doc Prothro feared Gray would never make it. The fans came out to see him play, though, and soon Pete began to respond like a professional. By the end of the 1943 season, he was playing regularly and batting .289.

In 1944, Pete became the best player in the Southern Association. He batted .333, stole 68 bases, tying the league record, and was voted the Most Valuable Player. But he was happiest about the five home runs he hit. One thing a one-armed batter would seem to lack is power, and he felt that these five home runs made him a complete ballplayer.

One day during the season, a man brought a one-armed boy to the park to see Pete play. "I'll show you how Pete Gray plays baseball," Pete promised the boy before the game.

He did everything he had promised. He made eight catches in the outfield, fielding his position perfectly.

The game went into extra innings, and when Pete came to bat in the twelfth, with his team one run behind, he had already made four hits.

He faced the Nashville pitcher with grim determination. He got a pitch he liked and swung hard with his 36-ounce bat. It was a line drive that sailed over the leftfielder's head. By the time the ball reached the infield again, Pete was on third base with a triple.

Gray's was the first of two runs that Memphis scored in the twelfth, winning the game. Pete had shown his young admirer that there was a place for handicapped people even in baseball.

Pete's greatest thrill was yet to come. His ambition had been to play in the major leagues. Scouts from many teams had watched him play in Memphis. Some of them had recommended him. The eight league managers had endorsed him as a major league prospect. Still, he went home to Nanticoke after the season in doubt about his future.

It wasn't long before the doubt was erased. The St. Louis Browns announced that they had bought Pete's contract from Memphis for 20,000 dollars. This was especially gratifying because the Browns had just won the American League pennant.

Throughout spring training the next year, Pete was a quiet withdrawn member of the Browns. He couldn't be sure that baseball wanted him for his

Until he proved himself with the Browns, one-armed Pete Gray was not sure whether he was wanted for his ability or his oddity.

ability rather than his oddity as a one-armed player. Manager Luke Sewell, a compassionate man, had tried to convince Pete that whatever job he earned would be because of his ability.

Pete played infrequently when the season opened. He was called upon for pinch-running, pinch-hitting and an occasional appearance in the outfield. In mid-

May the New York Yankees came to Sportsman's Park in St. Louis for a major series of the home season. On a bright Sunday afternoon, the two teams met for a double-header before a crowd of 21,000.

Pete reached the park that day with the uneasy feeling that had become habitual with him in St. Louis. He was afraid that someday he might walk into the clubhouse only to be told that he was being sent back to the minors.

He was just buttoning up his uniform when he saw Manager Sewell walking toward him.

"Pete," said the manager, clapping his player on the back. "You're my new lead-off man. You'll be playing right field."

This was a great moment in Pete Gray's life—playing right field and leading off against the New York Yankees.

Pete showed his appreciation to Sewell and the Browns on the field that afternoon. He got on base five times, had four hits, drove in two runs, scored two runs and made nine plays in the outfield. The Browns beat the Yankees twice.

At last, Pete Gray realized his ambition—to be a real major leaguer.

4
One Last Game

Jim O'Rourke just couldn't give up baseball. He had begun playing the game in 1866 at the age of fourteen on the sandlots of his hometown, Bridgeport, Connecticut. Thirty-eight years later, he was still playing with the enthusiasm of a young man, even though he was over fifty.

Jim had attracted the attention of the Middletown (Connecticut) Mansfields, one of the teams in the new professional league, and joined them when he was barely twenty years old. He played first base for the Boston Red Sox and impressed spectators with plays that are routine nowadays—one-handed catches and line-drive snags. His popularity in Boston produced a string of clamoring children wherever he went. He was one of early baseball's best fielders and heaviest hitters. O'Rourke was something of a showman, too. Before games he would often engage in juggling stunts with the other infielders. During the next twenty-five years, he had played nearly two thousand games for the Boston, Providence, Buffalo, New York and Washington teams.

Jim was one of those men who just wanted to play baseball. By the end of his career, he had played nearly every position on some major league team. During his four years in Buffalo (when that team was in the majors), he was the manager as well. But O'Rourke particularly liked to catch and it was as a catcher that he played his last big league game.

When Washington gave him his release in 1893, Jim O'Rourke was forty-one years old. But he refused to give up baseball. Instead, to make sure that he had a place to play, he went back to Bridgeport and organized the Connecticut League. Then he formed his own team in Bridgeport as a member of the new league.

In 1904 Jim was still catching and managing the Bridgeport team. He was fifty-two years old and was also the secretary-treasurer of the Connecticut League. Furthermore, on days when the grounds-keeper failed to show up, which happened frequently, old Jim put the playing field in condition.

In New York, in the 1904 season, the New York Giants were about to clinch the National League Pennant. It was their first championship since 1889, when Jim O'Rourke had been one of their big stars. Nearby in Bridgeport, Jim followed the Giants closely. As the Giants approached the pennant-winning game, he had an idea.

On the day before the Giants were to play the game in which they could clinch the pennant, Jim took a train to New York. He approached John McGraw, manager of the Giants, and told him that he wanted to play one more time in the big leagues, if only for an inning.

McGraw was a manager of the old school. He ran his team with an iron hand and seldom gave in to sentiment.

"But Jim," he said to O'Rourke, "you're fifty-two years old."

"That doesn't make any difference," O'Rourke said. "I catch every day in Bridgeport."

"It's out of the question," McGraw said. "You ought to know better than to ask."

Jim continued to plead, but McGraw stood firm. The Giants were playing Cincinnati the next day for their one hundredth victory of the season as well as for the pennant. McGraw felt that this was no time for sentimental gestures.

O'Rourke then thought of another angle. He heard that "Iron Man" Joe McGinnity was to pitch for the Giants. He knew Iron Man and went to talk with him. Iron Man knew that Jim O'Rourke would be a good catcher, regardless of his age. So he agreed to talk to McGraw for O'Rourke.

"He just wants to catch an inning, Mr. McGraw," McGinnity said to his manager. "What can it hurt? It'll give him a big kick and the fans will like it, too. Besides, if we lose the game, we'll win the next one. We're not going to lose this pennant now."

Finally, McGraw gave in. The next afternoon at New York's Polo Grounds, the battery for the Giants was McGinnity and O'Rourke—and no prouder man than Jim ever wore a big league uniform.

The first inning went so well that when Jim returned to the bench he said, "I feel so good I think I'd like to catch another inning."

McGraw consented to let him stay in the game. Two innings became three and then Jim came to bat. The crowd cheered him because he reminded them of earlier Giant successes. He got a pitch he liked and lashed it into left field. Rounding first, Jim saw the left fielder bobble the ball. So he headed for second. The throw to second was wild, and Jim steamed into third.

That did it. The veteran from Bridgeport caught the whole game, never letting one of Iron Man McGinnity's pitches get by him or making a wild throw. The Giants won the game, their one hundredth victory and the pennant, and to Jim O'Rourke it was just like old times in 1889.

He went back to Bridgeport the next day flushed with success. One game was enough. He had proved that Jim O'Rourke could still catch for a big league team. After the Giants had won the pennant, he reminded his friends that he had helped to win the deciding game. He had been on his first pennant winning team in 1873—thirty-one years earlier.

Just to prove that he was no one-game flash in

the pan, Jim O'Rourke caught for five more seasons
in Bridgeport before he finally let a younger man have
his place. He retired from baseball in 1909 at the
age of fifty-seven.

5

The Catcher Who Pitched All Night

Odell Barbary was never a famous player. He played only one game in the major leagues and never got a hit. He might have stayed in the majors much longer if he hadn't ruined his chances during a night game in Charlotte, North Carolina, in 1942.

Barbary was a catcher. By nature, he was a friendly country boy given to a lot of banter around the clubhouse. He was tall and lanky and had a long neck and strawberry-red hair. His teammates, the Charlotte Hornets of the Piedmont League, liked him because he could take a ribbing as well as he could hand one out.

On many occasions after a Charlotte pitcher turned in a sparkling performance, Barbary would needle him in his Southern drawl. "Man, you pitched tonight the way I used to pitch in high school," he would say. "It's a shame talent like mine has got to go to waste a-catchin'."

Some of the pitchers got angry, but most of them took it in good spirit. Barbary's boasting wasn't objectionable. For that matter, no one knew if he had ever pitched in his life. Therefore, few took him seriously.

One of the pitchers had a quick temper, however. "If you could catch as well as you say you can pitch," he said, "you'd be in the big leagues now."

Barbary only grinned and said, "I will be. You wait and see."

A few days before the end of the season, it happened. Barbary was bought by the Washington Senators and told to report for spring training the next year.

The pitcher began to press him now. "All right, big leaguer, now let's see you pitch."

"Aw, I hate to show you fellers up," Barbary replied.

By this time, the rest of the Hornets had joined in. They all wanted to see Barbary pitch.

In the game against Asheville on the final night of the season, Manager Harry Smythe gave his players a chance to play the position of their choice. Rising to his feet, Barbary said, "All right, gentlemen, you're going to see the great Barbary pitch tonight."

The Hornets cheered, and true to his word Barbary marched to the mound at Griffith Park in Charlotte. His pitching form wasn't very good, but he got the Asheville team out in the first inning with no trouble.

In the second inning, Asheville scored three runs. It was especially embarrassing when the Asheville pitcher, Larry Kempe, drove in two runs himself.

Barbary was unflustered, however, when he returned to the mound in the third inning. With the poise of a twenty-game winner, he shut out the Asheville team for two more innings. His teammates rallied in the fourth and tied the score, 3–3.

From this point on, Odell Barbary's pitching talent became a little more amazing each time he went out to pitch. The fifth, sixth, seventh, eighth and ninth innings went by and the score remained tied, 3 to 3.

In the tenth, it appeared that Barbary might be finished. Asheville put a runner on third base with only one out. But when the runner tagged up and tried to score on a fly to center field, the center fielder threw him out at the plate.

In the fourteenth inning, Charlotte had a chance to win. Charlotte's center fielder, the fastest runner in the league, singled and stole second. He moved to third on an infield out. But when he tried to score on a short fly to left field, he was cut down, in spite of his speed, by a good throw to the plate.

The fifteenth, sixteenth, seventeenth and eighteenth innings passed, and Barbary kept pitching. If anything, he was showing more style than at the beginning of the game, as if he was developing a rhythm. Fans who had been listening to a broadcast of the game began arriving at the park to see the miracle for themselves.

Finally, in the last half of the twenty-second inning, the end came suddenly. Charlie Roberts, the Charlotte shortstop, got a two-base hit. Smut Anderholt,

Odell Barbary boasted of his pitching ability, but no one took him very seriously.

who was playing third and had been to bat nine times without a hit, also doubled, and Roberts scored the run that made Odell Barbary the winning pitcher.

The catcher had pitched the longest game in the history of the Piedmont League. He had given up only eleven hits in twenty-two innings and scored the only two strikeouts of the game. But his boasting and his acceptance of his teammate's challenge were disastrous for him. Barbary ruined his great throwing arm that night, and with it he ruined his career.

Barbary was strangely humble in the clubhouse after the game that night. He said little and accepted congratulations with uncommon modesty. "I'll have to tell you the truth," he told his teammates after the crowd had retreated. "I never pitched a game before today in my life."

6

The "Miracle Braves" of 1914

Whenever sports comebacks are the topic of conversation the Boston Braves of 1914 are always mentioned. Saluting this determined team, Grantland Rice once wrote, "The Braves proved that no fight is hopeless."

Boston had finished fifth in the National League in 1913, to the severe displeasure of Manager George Stallings. Stallings was a hot-tempered Georgian who had no tolerance for defeat. One year he fired one of his players because he whistled a tune in the shower after losing a game.

"If a player is an easy loser," Stallings stormed, "I don't want him on my team."

Stallings always dressed in street clothes and wore out three or four pairs of trousers in a season, nervously sliding back and forth on the bench during the games. The 1914 season began on such a sour note that he was wearing out trousers as fast as his tailor could make them.

The Braves lost eighteen of their first twenty-two games and were unchallenged for last place. Baseball tradition says that the team in first place on July 4 will eventually win the pennant. But on July 4, the Braves were still last, fifteen games behind, and the New York Giants were leading the League.

As late as July 19, the Braves were still in eighth place. But Stallings had been making trades and the team was showing some new life. The Braves were

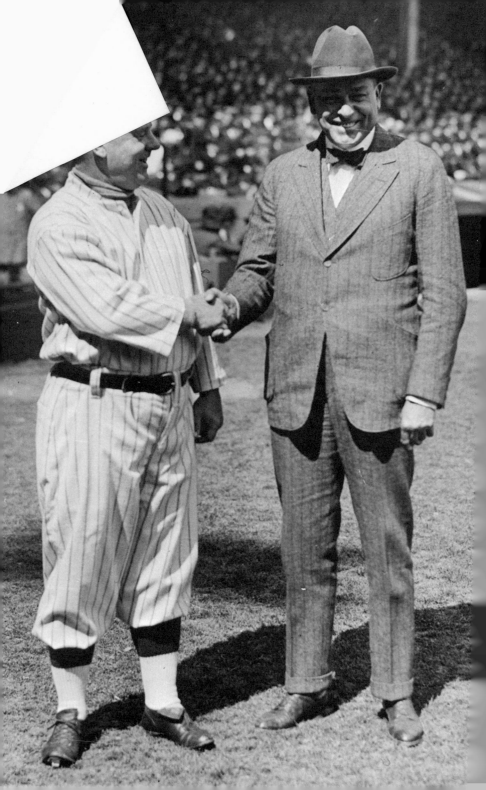

mostly players unwanted by other teams. Stallings added to their reputation as rejects when he picked up players from St. Louis, Philadelphia, Cincinnati and Brooklyn.

But the cast-offs from other clubs were soon proving their worth. By August, the Braves were really sailing. On August 10, they moved into second place, breathing down the Giants' necks. In early September they caught up with the Giants and passed them. In a key game of the series in which they overtook the Giants, the Braves won the hard way. They scored three runs off Christy Mathewson, one of the greatest pitchers of all time, and won in the last of the ninth inning, 5–4.

The Braves were not to be stopped. In the second half of the season, they won 60 games and lost only 16. They won the pennant by an amazing margin of 10½ games. But there was still a widespread tendency to call their triumph a fluke.

It is true that the Giants had fallen into a slump due to inferior pitching and the failure of some established veterans to play up to their past performances. But no one could deny that the Braves had played sensationally during the last half of the season. They probably would have been taken more seriously had they not been opposing the Philadelphia Athletics in the World Series.

*aves manager George Stallings, who always dressed in street clothes,
seen here with Giant manager, John McGraw.*

were the "New York Yankees" of that
line-up included five players who later
ted into the Cooperstown Hall of Fame:
ners Herb Pennock, Chief Bender and Ed Plank;
third baseman Frank "Home Run" Baker and second
baseman Eddie Collins. Jack Barry played shortstop
and Stuffy McInnis played first base, completing what
was known as the "Hundred-Thousand-Dollar Infield."
Manager Connie Mack was already considered one
of the greatest managers of all time. He had won
three of the four previous World Series.

Going into the 1914 World Series, then, the make-
shift Braves were considered certain to lose to the
vaunted American League champions. The National
Leaguers found themselves the subject of ridicule, in
spite of their dramatic rush to the pennant. When
asked if he had scouted the Braves, Chief Bender
reflected the feeling of the whole team with his
sarcastic answer. "There's no need scouting a bush-
league club like that."

There was some basis for the light regard in which
the Braves were held. The catcher, Hank Gowdy,
was only twenty-four and had never been a regular
player before. The pitching staff had a decided lack
of depth. For one of the pitchers, Bill James, this was
his only good season. He won only 37 games in the
majors, 26 of them in 1914.

Johnny Evers, the captain and shortstop, eventually made the Hall of Fame. But by 1914 he was a tired veteran having his last big moment. He never played a hundred games in a season again. The outfield was of such questionable quality that Stallings had used twelve men to play the three positions during the season and was still shuffling for the right combination in the World Series.

The first game was played in Philadelphia. The Braves' Dick Rudolph, a little right-hander weighing only 155 pounds, beat the Athletics and their famous pitcher, Chief Bender, 7–1. In the second game, James, who was to win only five more games in his major league career, beat the great Athletics pitcher Eddie Plank, 1–0, on a two-hitter. Afterward Mr. Mack coldly commented to Plank, "They play pretty well for bush leaguers, don't they, Eddie?"

As the teams switched from Philadelphia to Boston to resume the series, the Braves' clubhouse attendant asked Manager Stallings if he should leave the players' road uniforms in Philadelphia to save the trouble of transporting them back and forth.

"No," snapped Stallings. "We won't be coming back."

The opening game in Boston was one of the most thrilling World Series games ever played. The Braves' George Tyler faced the Athletics' Joe Bush, known

The Miracle Braves of 1914: 1. Gowdy, 2. James, 3 Evers, 4. Rudolph, 5. Tyler, 6. Connolly, 7. Moran, 8. Mann.

as "Bullet Joe," then only twenty-one years old.

The game went into extra innings, tied at 2–2. When the Athletics scored two runs in the top of the tenth, the outcome seemed certain. But as Grantland Rice wrote, "The Braves proved that no fight is hopeless."

Hank Gowdy, the Braves' young catcher, hit a home run to open the Braves' half of the inning. Then, Joe Connolly drove in Herb Moran on a sacrifice fly to tie the score 4–4. Boston fans were delirious.

The game wore on into the twelfth inning. In the Braves' half, Gowdy, who was having a tremendous series, came to bat. He hit a ground-rule double into the left-field bleachers and was then removed for a pinch runner, Les Mann. The next batter walked and Moran, the old cast-off from Cincinnati, laid down a bunt. "Bullet Joe" Bush pounced on the ball and had time to force Mann at third. But his hurried throw was wild, and Mann came home with the winning run. Final score: Braves 5, Athletics 4.

The fourth game was almost unnecessary. The proud Philadelphians were humbled and stumbling, desperately trying to regain their form. Stallings started Rudolph again, and by the fifth inning the little fellow had a 3–1 lead, which he carefully protected during the rest of the game.

Gowdy had batted .545, as well as winning fielding honors, and Rudolph and James had been the pitching stars. The mighty Athletics had lost four straight to Boston's "bush leaguers." It was the first time in modern baseball history that the losing team had not won at least one game. The miracle of the 1914 Braves was complete.

7

The Dog That Made a Box Score

A large Cuban baseball player named Roberto Gonzalo Ortiz appeared in Charlotte, North Carolina, in 1941, to play baseball for the Charlotte Hornets in the Piedmont League. Ortiz loved to play baseball and the Washington Senators, who owned his contract, thought he played very well. He came as a pitcher who had burning speed, but little control. When he started to play for the Hornets, he was switched to the outfield, where his strong arm would command respect of base runners.

Because Ortiz could barely speak English, he found himself alone in Charlotte except for one Cuban friend and a small dog, who was the color of cooked squash. The Cuban boy was shy but animals loved him, especially his homeless mongrel dog. When the team worked out, the yellow dog romped along with Ortiz. When the team went into the clubhouse, he seemed to wait especially for Ortiz to come out. When the team played, the yellow dog seemed to know that his place was out of the way.

Another thing the dog seemed to know was baseball. The excitement in the stands created when the Charlotte team would work up a rally excited him, too. Often the groundskeeper would be forced to chase him out of the park.

One Sunday afternoon, though, while the yellow dog was enjoying the freedom of the park, he completely forgot himself. Out of it he emerged as one of the most famous dogs in baseball lore.

The Charlotte team went to bat in the last of the ninth inning trailing by one run, apparently the victim of a tough pitcher. But the pitcher lost his control momentarily, and walked a Hornet batter. The next batter was Roberto Ortiz.

The big Cuban got a pitch that he liked and lashed into it. As he hit the ball, the crowd leaped to its feet with a roar. This aroused the yellow dog, who was sleeping in the dirt under the first-base bleachers. The ball had gotten by the center fielder and a run was scoring, tying the game. Ortiz would be trying for every base he could get.

As the Cuban neared first, he was joined by a sudden blur. The yellow dog, catching sight of his friend, had burst through the open clubhouse gate and was off to join him. Down to second base they went, the big Cuban and the little dog, running like a team. Then around second base, past the shortstop, whom the dog barely missed while making his wide turn.

The throw was coming in from the outfield now and Ortiz was in danger as he neared third. The coach signaled for him to slide and as Ortiz slid, the yellow dog slid, too. The umpire's hands flattened out in a safety signal. Both Ortiz and his dog had

Both Ortiz and his dog were safe at third.

made it.

How the game ended is really not important. What is important took place the next day. In the box score of the game, the Charlotte *News* made a special place for the little yellow dog. He appeared underneath Ortiz' name: "y—Yellow Dog." Below, in the space usually reserved for pinch hitters and pinch runners, appeared his explanatory line: "y—Yellow Dog ran with Ortiz in the 9th."

8
Corporal Brissie
and
Dr. Brubaker

Lou Brissie was seventeen years old and a freshman at Presbyterian College in South Carolina when the Japanese made their sneak attack at Pearl Harbor on December 7, 1941. The United States declared war, and immediately a fever to join the armed forces swept through college campuses. Brissie was one of those who felt the urge to volunteer.

But he had another ambition, too. He had always wanted to pitch for Connie Mack and the Philadelphia Athletics. Mack was the grand old man of baseball and had been the manager of the Athletics for more than forty years. Brissie's college coach, Eric McNair, a former Athletics shortstop, had seen Brissie pitch for the big mill team in his hometown, Ware Shoals, South Carolina, and had taken him to Philadelphia for a tryout with the Athletics. Brissie was tall and left-handed with a whip of a delivery in the style of the A's great Lefty Grove, who won three hundred games in the majors.

Mr. Mack had been impressed. But he advised Brissie to go to college and get an education. A contract with the Athletics would be waiting for him when he graduated. Mr. Mack even helped pay Brissie's college expenses, so the young man was especially eager to justify Mr. Mack's faith in him.

Then came World War II and Pearl Harbor; Brissie's guaranteed future began to collapse around him. Finally, in December, 1942, he could no longer resist the urge to enlist in the army.

"Coach, I've got to go," Brissie said to Eric McNair. "I'll be drafted sooner or later anyway. I want to go now so that I can get back to the Athletics and start pitching for Mr. Mack."

McNair knew that it would be of no use to try to stop him. Brissie was a boy of conscience and good judgment, and he had made up his mind.

Two years later, on December 7, 1944, in the Apennine Mountains of Italy, Corporal Lou Brissie and his fellow infantrymen were encamped near the city of Bologna. Brissie, now six feet, four inches tall and twenty years old, was leading a rifle squad on patrol.

Suddenly, with no warning, a self-propelled shell from German attackers struck near Brissie and his squad. Fragments flew everywhere, and not a member of Brissie's squad was left standing. Most of them were killed; the others were critically wounded.

How long he lay there, Brissie never knew. Slowly, though, consciousness returned. He could smell the acrid smoke that hung over the ravine in which he lay. He could see, though his vision was dull and shimmery, but he couldn't talk or move.

His first thoughts were of survival, and when a

searching party arrived this seemed assured. But the
searching party started to pass him by. They thought
he was dead, like the rest, and he couldn't cry out
to let them know he was alive. He tried, but he
had lost his voice, a temporary condition brought on
by shock.

"Hey, that one moved!" one of the searching party
said, taking one last glance at the mangled rifle
squadsmen.

Somehow, through desperate effort, Brissie had
moved his body enough to get one man's attention.
Otherwise, he would have been left for dead. He had
already lain in that muddy ravine for more than six
hours, the shinbone of his left leg shattered by a
piece of the shell, his body riddled with fragments.
The fact that he had lived through the December
chill and the loss of blood was a miracle in itself, but
the miracles were only beginning.

At the battalion first-aid station, Brissie was given
the first of forty blood transfusions. The next stop
was the evacuation hospital in Naples, where Brissie
woke up one morning to find a doctor bending over
him, saying to an aide:

"This leg will have to come off."

Corporal Brissie now made the greatest stand of
his life. Struggling into a leaning position on one
elbow, he protested, "You can't take my leg off, doctor!

I'm a baseball player, and I've got to play ball."

The doctor, Major Wilbur Brubaker, was a serious man who seldom smiled or talked. By coincidence, he was also an ardent fan of the Cleveland Indians. Naturally, he had never heard of Lou Brissie, but the boy's determination convinced Brubaker to dedicate himself to making it possible for him to play baseball again.

There was not a piece of bone more than four inches long left in Brissie's leg. The idea that a pitcher as heavy as Lou would ever again be able to pivot and throw off the shattered leg seemed incredible but Major Brubaker offered him cautious encouragement. He warned Brissie, however, that complete recovery would take time and perseverance.

Putting Brissie's shattered leg back together again was like fitting together the pieces of a jigsaw puzzle. Major Brubaker used pieces of the fractured bone and wire and patience. He also had to fight the infection brought on by Brissie's long exposure to the cold.

After that it was a matter of one operation after another and one hospital after another for Corporal Brissie. First he went to the 300th General Evacuation Hospital in Naples. Then he was returned to the United States, where he was assigned to Finney General Hospital in Thomasville, Georgia. Next he went to Northington General Hospital in Tuscaloosa, Alabama, and finally he was transferred to Valley Forge General Hospital in Valley Forge, Pennsylvania.

He underwent twenty-three operations. But because of Major Brubaker's skill, the crisis had already passed and the leg had been saved. Strength was returning, though Brissie still had to use a crutch to get about. Since he was close to Philadelphia, he began to think about calling on Connie Mack and letting him know that his pitcher was on the way.

Throughout Brissie's time in the service, Mr. Mack had corresponded with him. After the battlefield injury, Mr. Mack's letters became more frequent and reassuring. "There will always be a place for you with the Athletics," Mr. Mack wrote soon after Brissie's brush with death. "Your first order is to recover and to keep your courage high. Then when you are well again, we shall have your uniform ready."

Mr. Mack's encouragement, Brissie's own desire to play baseball again and the faith of fellow patients who knew about his ambitions helped pull Lou through many periods of deep depression.

Finally the moment arrived. One morning in July, 1946, a tall, broad-shouldered young man with a crutch under his left arm presented himself at the offices of the Philadelphia Athletics. He said to the receptionist, "Tell Mr. Mack that Lou Brissie is here."

The uniform was ready, just as Mr. Mack had

promised. Brissie wore it that day and even warmed up with the bull-pen catcher. He stumbled about uncertainly and almost fell down trying to throw. The idea that this poor fellow would ever throw a baseball in the American League seemed absurd. Mr. Mack, however, patted him on the back and gave him more reassurance.

A few days later, Brissie returned to Valley Forge Hospital for another operation. An infection had been brought on by his exertion in Philadelphia. In the office of the Athletics, many thought they had seen the last of Lou Brissie as a baseball player.

Imagine their surprise when he arrived at their spring training camp in Florida the next year vibrantly healthy and ready to play. Over the damaged leg he now wore a steel brace and a lightweight shinguard similar to that worn by catchers. Although he was not as agile as most other players, he got about admirably for a man with only one good leg.

The Athletics had a farm team in Savannah, Georgia, and Mr. Mack decided that this was where his Purple Heart winner should break in. "You have shown me that you've got courage and you have shown me that you can pitch, Mr. Brissie," said Mr. Mack. "That's all I needed to know. One day you shall pitch for Philadelphia."

On opening day in the South Atlantic League in

Connie Mack's faith in Lou Brissie was justified when Lou signed a contract with the Athletics in 1948.

April, 1947, Lou Brissie was the starting pitcher for Savannah. At first things did not go well at all. The opposing team knocked him out of the box after four innings, but Savannah managed to win anyway.

Next came a defeat by Augusta, 3–0, and another defeat by Charleston, 1–0. Brissie was pitching well enough to win, and there was no doubt about the durability of the damaged leg, or his ability to perform on it. But his teammates just weren't hitting well enough.

In his fourth starting assignment, Brissie faced the Greenville team. Ware Shoals, Brissie's home town, is not far from Greenville, and that night many of his townspeople came to see him pitch. As he recognized old friends in the crowd, he filled with excitement.

Brissie beat Greenville that night and he didn't lose another game until July. Thirteen times in a row he won, and when the season was over, his record was 23 won and 5 lost. He had struck out 278 men in 254 innings, and achieved an earned run average of 1.91. He was the leading pitcher in the league in nearly every category.

In 1948 Philadelphia opened the American League season in Boston on Patriots Day. Connie Mack honored his returned war heroes by starting Phil Marchildon, a Canadian veteran, in the first game of

Lou was as determined on the pitching mound as he was on the battlefield.
He pitched successfully in the majors for six seasons.

the holiday double-header and former Corporal Lou
Brissie in the second game. Marchildon pitched well
and won a close game, 5–4.

The second game had been going only a few minutes when Brissie found himself pitching to one of
the best hitters baseball had ever known—Ted Williams, the Red Sox left fielder. It was the first time
Lou had ever seen the great Williams.

Although Brissie pitched carefully to him, the Red
Sox slugger got a pitch he liked and rifled it back
directly at the A's pitcher. Worse than that, the
drive struck Brissie's leg with such force that the ball
rolled all the way to the right-field fence.

Brissie fell as if he had been shot and players from
both teams crowded around him. All of them were
familiar with the story of the war hero's courageous
fight to pitch again, as were thousands in the stands
at Fenway Park.

Williams himself tagged base and anxiously joined
the crowd around the fallen pitcher. Looking up from
where he lay and spotting Williams' famous face
above him, Brissie smiled broadly.

"Williams," he said good-naturedly, "I thought you
were a pull-hitter."

A smile spread across Williams' face, too, and the
anxiety was dispelled.

"I knew then," Williams said later, "that that guy

would make it."

The steel brace and the shinguard had saved the wounded leg. Suffering only a bruise, Brissie got up and pitched the entire game. He beat the Red Sox, 3–2.

It was the start of a good career with the Athletics. Brissie won fourteen games that season and sixteen the next season. He pitched in the majors for six full seasons. The ambition of a man who refused to give up on the battlefield, in the hospital or on the playing field had been fulfilled.

9

The Midget of St. Louis

One morning in August, 1951, Bill Veeck, president of the St. Louis Browns, called a theatrical agent in Chicago and said, "Marty, I want you to find me a midget who's athletic and game for anything."

A few days later, Eddie Gaedel showed up in Veeck's office in St. Louis. Gaedel met all Veeck's specifications. He stood just three feet, seven inches tall, weighed only sixty-seven pounds and was athletically inclined. Veeck told Gaedel his plan, and found that the midget was quite willing to go through with it.

Veeck, who formerly operated the Cleveland Indians and later the Chicago White Sox, was known for his odd publicity schemes. He had used clowns in the coaching box. He had introduced Satchel Paige, a famed Negro pitcher, to the major leagues at the age of forty-eight, when most players have retired. He had awarded a ton of coal, a barrel of oysters and a billy goat as gate prizes.

After they had discussed Veeck's plan, Veeck sent Gaedel home to Chicago and told him to be back in St. Louis on Aug. 18. On that date, the Browns, the eighth-place team in the league, were playing the Detroit Tigers, the seventh-place team. Eighteen thousand fans were attracted to Sportsman's Park by a special day dedicated to one of the Browns' radio sponsors. Any fan could have detected on his score-

Bill Veeck (right) bought the Browns from Bill DeWitt (left), only a month before he introduced his midget to beef up the poor attendance.

card the addition of a player listed as "1/8: Gaedel." For some reason or another, few of them did. To those who did notice it, it looked like a typographical error.

Meantime, Veeck and his chief assistant, Bill Durney, had signed Gaedel to a formal American League player contract. In the secrecy of their office, they had schooled the midget in the technique of batting. And they had ordered the construction of a huge make-believe cake, supposedly as a part of the tribute to the radio sponsor.

A double-header was scheduled that Sunday afternoon. At the end of the between-games ceremony, the make-believe cake was rolled up to home plate. Out of the cake emerged Eddie Gaedel, dressed in an authentic St. Louis player uniform with the fractional number "1/8" on his back. To complete the costume, he wore a pair of elves' shoes turned up at the toes. He was a real, live Brownie.

Gaedel carried a toy bat, but no one suspected what was about to take place until the public-address announcer introduced the lead-off batter for the Browns in the last half of the first inning.

"Now batting for Saucier," he said in his ball-park baritone, "number 1/8, Gaedel."

Out of the St. Louis dugout strode Eddie Gaedel, carrying the toy bat on his tiny shoulder. The astonished umpire, Ed Hurley, took off his mask and called for the St. Louis manager, Zack Taylor.

"Hey, Zack," Hurley said, "what do you think you're doing? Is this some kind of joke?"

With a straight face, Taylor pulled an American League contract from his pocket showing that Eddie Gaedel had been duly signed to play for the St. Louis Browns at a salary of one hundred dollars a game. There was nothing Hurley could do but allow the midget to take his turn at bat.

Bob Swift, the Detroit catcher, called time. Bewildered, he walked to the mound and stood scratching his head as he and the Detroit pitcher, Bob Cain,

It was impossible for Detroit pitcher Bob Cain to pitch into a 1½ inch strike zone.

discussed the problem of pitching to a midget. Veeck had already measured Gaedel's "strike zone." It was 1½ inches high when Gaedel took the normal batting stance.

Veeck had ordered Gaedel not to swing at a pitch under any condition. Realizing that no pitcher could throw three strikes through a 1½-inch zone, Veeck only wanted Gaedel to get a walk. Even without swinging at a pitch, he would bring national attention to the Browns, who were the poorest members of the American League, both in dollars and talent.

Gaedel was nervous as he stepped into the batter's box. He timidly took a stance in the left rear corner of the right-hand batting rectangle. Cain, a right-handed pitcher, still wore an expression of astonishment as he prepared to pitch. Catcher Swift unconsciously added to the hilarity of the situation by getting down on both knees behind the plate.

Cain's first pitch was a serious attempt at a strike. It sailed high over Gaedel's head. So did the second.

Now Cain was laughing. The next two pitches were just medium-hard lobs three feet over the midget's head. The little batter threw down his toy bat in the best professional manner and trotted down to first base.

Time was called while a pinch runner, Jim Delsing, was sent into the game for him. Again in the character of a professional player, Gaedel slapped Delsing across his rump as his replacement relieved him on first base.

Gaedel ran off the field, into the St. Louis dugout and out of the major leagues for life while 18,000 fans roared with laughter at the comedy they had witnessed.

The event had its repercussions. But despite complaints from baseball executives and some newspapers, Bill Veeck's publicity stunt was successful. He had brought badly needed attention to the St. Louis Browns, and he had brought off an act that will be talked about as long as baseball is played in America.

Eddie Gaedel had, in his own small way, also achieved the fame he sought. He would always be known as the only midget who ever played in the major leagues. Even Frank Saucier had set some kind of record. He was the only major leaguer ever to be taken out of a game for a midget.

10
Dusty Rhodes Breaks Up the Series

Leo Durocher once said that Dusty Rhodes was the craziest looking ballplayer he had ever seen. He wore his cap at a cockeyed angle. He ran with the speed of a weary blacksmith. His fielding was very uncertain. And for a throwing arm, he might as well have been using a rubber band. But he could hit.

Because Dusty Rhodes could hit, the New York Giants, managed by Durocher, won the National League pennant in 1954. At the two most critical points of the season, in a series against the Brooklyn Dodgers, it was Rhodes' pinch hits that led the Giants to victory. Playing mostly as a pinch hitter and a reserve outfielder, Rhodes went to bat only 164 times during the regular season. But he hit 15 home runs and drove in 50 runs while compiling an average of .341.

But this was only the warm-up for the grand finale. In the 1954 World Series the Giants met the Cleveland Indians. The Indians had a team of historic strength, including Early Wynn, Mike Garcia, Bob Lemon and the great Bob Feller as starting pitchers and the best relievers in the major leagues—Ray Narleski and Don Mossi. They had won 111 games during the season, a record for the American League.

The Giants were not a spectacular team, but they were well balanced. Johnny Antonelli and Sal Maglie were the pitching stars and Willie Mays, Al Dark and

Don Mueller lead the offense. Dusty Rhodes was in reserve.

The series began in New York, and the Indians were favored to beat the Giants on the strength of their pitching. Lemon, who had won twenty-three games during the regular season, was facing Maglie, who had won only fourteen. Cleveland scored two runs in the first inning, but the Giants tied the game in the third. From that point until the tenth inning, it was a pitchers' duel. In the eighth inning, Willie Mays saved the Giants from defeat when he made a spectacular catch against the wall in center field. Two Indians were on base at the time and would almost certainly have scored if Mays had missed the ball.

When the Giants came up in the last half of the tenth, the score was still 2–2. Mays walked and stole second. Hank Thompson was walked intentionally. It was Monte Irvin's turn to bat when Durocher put in his first call for Rhodes to pinch hit.

Rhodes came out of the dugout with his slew-footed walk, swinging an armful of bats. He stepped in to face Lemon and looked at only one pitch. He knocked it into the right-field bleachers at the Polo Grounds, driving in three runs. The Giants won, 5–2.

In the second game, Cleveland led 1–0 going into the Giants' half of the fifth inning. Mays walked and Thompson reached base behind him on a single.

Dusty is being congratulated on his 10th-inning three-run homer in the 1954 Series against the Indians.

Irvin would be up next. As Durocher recounted it later, "I looked down the bench and there was Dusty, already up with a bat in his hand. He didn't say anything, but his eyes said, 'Put me in, Skip. I'm ready.' And so I put him in."

This time Rhodes faced Early Wynn, who was then at the peak of a fine career. He slapped a single into right field, scoring Mays. Thompson scored later, and the Giants led, 2–1.

After batting for Irvin, Rhodes went to left field in Irvin's place. Coming to bat in the seventh inning, Dusty gave the Giants a safe lead with a smashing home run that hit the facing on the upper deck of the Polo Grounds.

The Series moved to Cleveland for the third game, where Mike Garcia faced Ruben Gomez of the Giants. The Giants got to Garcia early, with singles by Dark and Mueller opening the third inning. An intentional walk loaded the bases, and Irvin was due at bat. It was early, but there was little hesitation now. Rhodes was up with a bat in his hand again. This time he needed only one pitch. He drove another single into right field, scoring two runs. The Giants won again 6–1.

The next day the Giants took the Series from the Indians with their fourth straight victory, completing one of the great upsets of the year.

Durocher managed to win the fourth game without calling on Rhodes. But the confident utility man had already done enough for one World Series. In six times at bat, he delivered four hits for an average of .667. He hit two home runs and drove in seven runs. Three of his hits and one of his home runs had come when he was a pinch hitter.

This incredible record marked the pinnacle of a short-lived baseball career. After the series Rhodes was acclaimed one of the game's most exciting performers and yet three years later, at the age of thirty, he was back in the minor leagues. But for one four-game World Series there has never been a hotter man with a bat than Dusty Rhodes.

11

A Game
of
Records

The World Series of 1920 set a number of records. First, Cleveland had never played in a modern World Series. Their opponents, the Brooklyn Dodgers, had played in the series just four years earlier but had been in the second division ever since. It was a surprise that the two teams were there at all. But it was the fifth game that kept the record keepers busy.

Twenty-six thousand fans crowded into old League Park in Cleveland to see the two teams play that day. The Series was tied at two victories apiece. Each manager was starting his pitching ace: Burleigh Grimes for Brooklyn and Jim Bagby for Cleveland. Grimes had beaten Bagby in the second game so Bagby was particularly eager to win the rematch.

From the first inning the Indians began giving Grimes double trouble. The first two Indian batters reached base on singles. Then, Tris Speaker, the Indians' player-manager laid down a bunt, and as Grimes attempted to field it, he fell flat on his back. The bases were loaded with nobody out when Elmer Smith came to bat. Some fans were still trying to find their seats in the midst of this hubbub. Smith had batted over .300 in 1920 for the first time since 1914 when he had appeared in only 13 games.

Grimes bore down on the Indian batter, who swung at the first two pitches and missed. The third pitch was outside as Grimes "wasted" one, and Smith let

Elmer Smith

it go by. But the fourth pitch was a fast ball that was just what Smith had been waiting for. He swung and the ball disappeared over the right-field screen.

The three base runners spun around the bases, followed by Elmer Smith, who had done something no other player had ever done. It was the first grand-slam home run hit in a World Series. To prove that it was no simple feat, thirty-three years passed before Mickey Mantle of the Yankees hit the next series grand-slammer against the Dodgers in 1953.

Grimes was still pitching as the fourth inning began. The Indians threatened again. The lead-off man, Doc Johnston, got a hit, took second on a passed ball and went to third on an infield out. Steve O'Neill, the catcher, was walked because Bagby, who was the next batter, was a weaker hitter and Grimes figured he could handle him. Instead, Bagby slammed a drive into right-center field that fell into the bleachers for a three-run home run, the first home run ever hit in a World Series by a pitcher.

By the fifth inning, Grimes had disappeared from the game. The merciless Indians had hammered him for nine hits and seven runs, including the two historic home runs and a triple. Working with such a comfortable lead, the Indians' Bagby seemed to let up in the fifth. The first two Dodger batters, Pete Kilduff and Otto Miller led off with singles, bringing up Grimes' replacement, pitcher Clarence Mitchell. With runners on first and second and no one out, the Dodger manager was willing to allow his pitcher to bat rather than call on a pinch hitter. In fact, he felt so much confidence in Mitchell that he flashed the hit-and-run sign, meaning that both Kilduff and Miller were to be off and running as Bagby released his pitch.

Mitchell met the ball squarely for what seemed to be a certain hit over second base. Since Dodger base runners were moving, Wambsganss, the Indian second baseman, ran toward second base to cover on the play. With an acrobatic leap, Wambsganss speared the line drive for one out. Suddenly he

Bill Wambsganss.

found himself faced with the play of a lifetime.

Kilduff, who had been on second base, was already nearing third. Wambsganss stepped on second base, forcing Kilduff out for the second out. Miller, who had been on first base, was nearing second when he realized what was happening and came to a dead stop. Wambsganss simply put the tag on him for the third out. He had completed the first and only unassisted triple play in World Series history.

It was no more Mitchell's day at bat than it had

been Grimes' day on the mound. The next time the Brooklyn relief pitcher came to bat, a teammate was on first base. He hit another smashing ball, this time on the ground, to Wambsganss, who promptly turned it into a double play. In two times at bat, Mitchell had been responsible for five of his team's outs. This was another first in a World Series.

Five victories were required to win a World Series in those days. The Dodgers were so thunderstruck by the Indians' performance in the fifth game that they never recovered. They lost that day, 8–1, and never scored another run as the Indians shut them out twice and completed the Series in two more days.

12

Ol' Diz Makes a "Comeback"

In the mid-1930s, Dizzy Dean was one of the greatest pitchers baseball had ever seen. But by 1938, he was through. The St. Louis Cardinals, for whom he had had his biggest years, had traded him to the Chicago Cubs. The Cubs used him sparingly in 1938, just enough to help them win the pennant, but he was pitching with his heart and his head. His fast ball was gone.

Dean struggled through two more seasons with the Cubs, then suffered the humiliation of being sent down to the minor leagues. The best he could do with Tulsa in the Texas League was to break even, winning eight and losing eight.

This was the final confirmation. Even Dean was forced to admit that he was through, and when the St. Louis Browns asked him to become their radio broadcaster in 1941, Dean accepted gladly. Talking had always been one of his strong points, but he usually talked about himself.

Talking about others was the unnatural part of baseball broadcasting for Dean, but in his unique way he learned to keep his listeners entertained. His grammar was so bad, however, that school teachers complained about his broadcasts. They said that he was a bad influence on their students. Although his use of the English language never improved, Dean did make himself valuable to the Browns, who were consistently the worst team in the American League.

Surprisingly, the Browns improved enough to win their first pennant in 1944, during World War II. But when the soldiers and sailors began returning home, strengthening the other teams in the league, the Browns slipped back into the second division. By 1947 they were dragging along in last place and attracting few fans to Sportsman's Park.

Bill DeWitt, president of the Browns, asked Dean to talk up the good plays the Browns made and keep their minds off the bad ones.

"Doggone it, Mr. DeWitt," Dean replied, "they just ain't making many good plays that I can talk about, but I'll try."

Try as he would, however, Dean frequently had to talk more about bird dogs, country recipes and country ballads than about the good plays the Browns were making. One day he became so disgusted with the Browns' pitchers that he blurted out: "Whatsa matter with these guys? Their fast balls wouldn't break a pane of glass. Doggone if I know what this game's comin' to. I'll bet I could beat nine out of ten of these guys that call theirselfs pitchers these days."

Among those listening to the broadcast were the wives of the Browns' pitchers. All of them were anxious about the welfare and reputations of their

Dizzy's remarks about the Browns' pitching angered the pitchers' wives.

husbands. They began calling President DeWitt and complaining.

"If that Dean thinks he's so great," they said, "why doesn't he get out there and pitch himself?"

DeWitt decided that the wives had a good idea. Attendance at the Browns' games was so low and debts were so high that he was willing to try anything that might bring out a crowd at Sportsman's Park.

He called Dean in.

"How would you like to pitch a game for the Browns, Diz?" asked DeWitt.

"I knowed that's what you wuz callin' me about," Dean said. "These females have been wearing me out on the telephone. I'm ready. When do I pitch?"

Dean went through the formality of signing a contract, which is necessary before appearance in a major league game. Then, on the afternoon of September 28, he left his broadcasting booth to pitch for the Browns. This was seven years after his last full season in baseball.

Dean faced the Chicago White Sox and, as DeWitt had expected, a crowd of 16,000 turned out for a game that normally would have drawn about 2,000. Don Kolloway, the White Sox first baseman, was the first batter Dean faced, and he lined a single into the outfield. The next batter hit into a double play and the third batter grounded out. Dean had survived the first inning.

In the second inning Dean gave up a single and a walk with one out. The wives of the Browns' pitchers must have been delighted. It looked as if Dean was about to be repaid for his unkind remarks about their husbands. But crafty old Diz had a few good pitches left. He kicked his left leg a little higher, reared back a little farther and threw to the

ven years after his last full season the Diz showed his old form again.

next batter. The batter hit a grounder to the short-stop, who flipped to second, starting another double play and ending the inning.

In the third inning, Dean put the White Sox down in order—Mike Tresh, Ed Lopat and Kolloway. Now it was time for Dizzy himself to come to bat. As Dean came down the dugout steps, Dutch Hofmann, one of the Browns' coaches, said, "Are you all right, Diz, or should I put a pinch hitter in for you now?"

"You're doggone right I'm all right," Dean told Hoffmann. "Where's my bat?"

Dean went to the plate swinging a red-striped bat made especially for him. When Pitcher Lopat of the White Sox delivered the ball, he swung. It was a hit, a line-drive single to left field. On the way to first, though, Dean pulled a muscle in his leg.

He did his best to cover up as he went back to the mound for the fourth inning, but he was plainly favoring the injured leg. The first batter singled, but Diz retired the next three. Even so, when he walked off the mound at Sportsman's Park at the end of the inning, he knew he'd pitched his last game.

"I guess I better let somebody else pitch, Dutch," Dean told Hofmann. "This leg of mine is about to kill me."

But Dean had proved his point. He had faced only fourteen batters in four innings, two above minimum, and had held the White Sox scoreless. The Browns didn't win, unfortunately. A relief pitcher lost the game in the ninth inning, but the defeat had nothing to do with Dizzy Dean.

"I said I could pitch as good as most of these fellers," Dean told newspapermen that day, "and I can. But I'll be doggoned if I'm gonna ever try again. Talking's my game now, and I'm just glad that muscle I pulled wasn't in my throat."

13

The One-Inning Home Run King

The *Official Baseball Guide* for 1930 shows that during that season a player named Gene Rye hit twenty-six home runs for Waco, Texas. But the record doesn't show that Rye, in that same season, also had the biggest inning a batter has ever had in professional baseball.

Rye's real name was Eugene Mercantelli. But before he left his home in Chicago to try his hand at the game, a friend convinced him that a long name like Mercantelli would never fit into a newspaper headline or a box score. So he changed his name to Gene Rye. Gene was almost as short as his new name, but he was a strong little man and his bowed legs gave him good balance in the batter's box.

Night baseball had just come to Waco in 1930, so when the club scheduled a night game on August 6, there was a good crowd at the stadium. An even larger audience followed the game by radio, for this was the first night game broadcast in the Texas League.

When Gene Rye reached the ball park that night, he felt no better or worse than usual. He had had a good season at Waco. He was batting among the league leaders and he had hit nearly twenty home runs. He was almost certain to be bought by a team in a higher league at the end of the season. Perhaps even the major leagues would be interested.

That night Waco was playing the Beaumont, Texas, team. Going into the eighth inning, Waco was behind, 6–2, and the Beaumont pitcher, Jerry Mallet, showed no signs of losing his sharpness.

Rye was the first batter of the inning for Waco, and he hit Mallet's second pitch over the right-field fence for a home run. One home run should not have affected the Beaumont team since they still had a three-run lead, but it seemed to affect Mallet. He gave up a walk, a single and another walk to the next three batters. Waco now had enough runners on base to tie the score, and Mallet was taken out.

A pitcher named Ed Green relieved him, but Green was no improvement. Waco not only tied the score, but runs began pouring across the plate as if a dike had broken. By the time the Beaumont manager called time again, seven runs had scored and there was not even one out. He brought in a third pitcher, Walter Newman.

The first batter Newman faced was Gene Rye. There were two men on base when Rye stepped in to bat for the second time in the inning. The swarthy little outfielder swung his bat, met Newman's pitch with a loud crack and sent another drive over the right-field fence.

Now ten runs had scored and Beaumont had not retired one Waco batter. They finally got one man out, but the parade of batters continued. Another player, Tony Piet, later an infielder with several major league teams, hit a home run. Then Pitcher Newman struck out a Waco player named Sanguinet for the second out. But the two outs weren't enough to keep Gene Rye from making a third appearance before the end of the inning. This time the bases were loaded. The crowd sat forward in the stands, eager to see what would happen.

The first pitch was a ball. With the bases loaded, Newman took a long windup. Then he threw again. Rye met the ball solidly and the fans jumped to their feet. The ball sailed over the head of the center fielder, over the fence in center field and out of the park, farther than either of the other two home runs.

By the time the inning ended, Waco had scored eighteen runs. Gene Rye had hit three home runs and driven in seven runs. In the press box, sports writers searched the pages of their record books to find another professional player who had ever hit three home runs in one inning, but found none. And no professional player since 1930 has equaled Gene Rye's performance.

Later that season the Boston Red Sox bought Rye's contract for 1931. Due to a knee injury, his career with the Red Sox lasted only seventeen games, however, during which he never hit a home run. There

was no place for him in the big league sun, but down in Waco, Texas, they continued to talk about Gene Rye—the man who swung a bat for one inning as no one has swung one before or since.

August 6, 1930, Gene Rye swung a bat for one inning as no one ever before or since. He is shown here with the Red Sox, who bought his ract that season.

14
The Day the Tigers Struck

The most untalented, unbelievable team that ever played major league baseball took the field in Philadelphia on May 18, 1912. The players wore the uniforms of the Detroit Tigers, but it didn't take close inspection to reveal that there wasn't a real Tiger in the group.

This team took the field as a result of the only strike that has ever been held in the major leagues. The strike had developed two days earlier in New York. On May 16, the Tigers played the New York Highlanders (later called the Yankees) in New York City. During the game, the constant heckling of one Highlander fan began to get on the nerves of the Tiger's hot-tempered star, Ty Cobb.

Once during the game, Cobb went to Harry Wolverton, manager of the Highlanders, and said, "There's going to be trouble if that fellow isn't stopped."

It is the home team's responsibility to maintain order in any park. But Cobb was given no assurance that measures would be taken to silence the man.

Finally, as Cobb was nearing his boiling point, the fan launched into another great outburst. Cobb sprinted for the stands, leaped the rail and picked out the abusive fan. By the time bystanders separated the men, the heckler was seriously cut and bruised.

Ban Johnson, president of the American League, suspended Cobb indefinitely without a hearing for

Cobb's suspension caused a Tigers' sympathy strike.

his behavior. But the Detroit players backed Cobb unanimously and sent Johnson the following telegram.

> Feeling Mr. Cobb is being done an injustice by your action in suspending him, we, the undersigned, refuse to play in another game until such action is adjusted to our satisfaction. He was fully justified, as no one could stand such personal abuse from any-one. We want him reinstated or there will be no game. If players cannot have protection, we must protect ourselves.

Detroit had an open date between the Highlander game and their game with Philadelphia on May 18. Meanwhile, Johnson came to Philadelphia from his office in Chicago and threatened the entire Detroit ball club with suspension if the players refused to take the field against the Athletics. Johnson also threatened the owner of the Tigers with a $5,000 fine for every game his team missed. To avoid the fine in case his team still refused to play, the owner instructed his manager, Hughey Jennings, to round up a standby team.

On May 17, word was passed around Philadelphia that Detroit was seeking a standby team. On the morning of May 18, an assortment of college and sandlot ballplayers showed up at the Aldine Hotel, Tiger headquarters in Philadelphia, hoping to play for the striking Tigers.

The hopeful recruits filed by in a long line while Jennings cut the "squad" by tapping good prospects on the shoulder. He interviewed them briefly and selected eighteen to fill the Detroit uniforms. He had a full squad ready in case the regular Tigers carried out their strike threat.

On the afternoon of May 18, the regular Tigers left their hotel rooms, went by taxi to Shibe Park, home of the Athletics, and suited up. Their spokesman, Jim Delahanty, asked the umpire in chief:

"Has Cobb's suspension been lifted?"

When the umpire told him it hadn't, the Tigers went back to the dressing room, removed their uniforms and returned to the hotel. The first and only major league baseball strike had begun.

At game time, Manager Jennings put his emergency team on the field. A young theology student from St. Joseph's College named Al Travers was selected to pitch. The third baseman was a local boxer who had reversed the letters of his last name, Graham, and was known as Billy Maharg.

Two loyal Tiger coaches were pressed into service, Joe Sugden and James McGuire. Sugden was forty-two years old and he had broken into the big leagues nearly twenty years before. He played first base. McGuire was approaching fifty and had been a player and manager in the majors for thirty years. He was the catcher. The rest of the team was filled out by students from St. Joseph's and Georgetown University and sandlotters from around Philadelphia.

The true identity of the player who filled Cobb's shoes in center field was not known for many years. All that came out in the newspaper box scores the next day was this abbreviation: "L'n'h's'r, cf." The man's name was Leinhauser and he later became a police officer in Philadelphia.

But anonymity was just as well for "L'n'h's'r" and all the others because the substitute Tigers were devastated. Jack Coombs, the pitching ace of the Athletics, started the game. He was succeeded in early innings by another pitcher named Boardwalk Brown, who allowed the pickups their only two runs of the game, produced chiefly by the two old coaches, Sugden and McGuire, who had one hit apiece, and a sandlot player named Irwin, who hit two triples in three times at bat.

Meanwhile, the Athletics scored at least two runs in every inning except the second and fourth. Eddie Collins, the Hall of Fame second baseman, made five hits and scored four runs. Amos Strunk, the center fielder, made four hits, including a double and a triple.

In the end, the Athletics got 25 hits off the unfortunate Travers and won the game 24–2. Travers, who later became a Roman Catholic priest, set a major league record by allowing 24 runs to score. It wasn't all his fault though: nine errors by his teammates accounted for ten unearned runs.

After the game, the problem of the strike still had to be solved. It was obvious that Detroit couldn't afford to put such an inept team on the field again, and there was another game to be played the next day. The striking Tigers weren't budging and Johnson remained firm.

Newspapermen from all over the league rushed to the scene to cover the story. In New York the *Daily American* conducted a poll among its readers, asking them if they favored Cobb or the League President. The vote resulted in a landslide for Cobb: 3,013 to 1,167. Mail poured in from aroused fans. Many who had been sitting close to the abusive fan in Highlander Park wrote of their sympathy for Cobb.

Finally, Cobb himself broke the deadlock. When it became clear that neither Johnson nor the Tigers would give in, Cobb went to his teammates and said:

"Boys, the principle of this thing has been entirely open to the public. I'm going to ask you to forget me and go back.

"I don't want you paying fines and one of the conditions of your going back should be that no fine will be enforced on any of you. I'll be all right. They'll let me come back sometime soon, so please go back and play tomorrow."

As soon as Johnson reduced Cobb's suspension to ten days and established his fine at fifty dollars, the Detroit players returned to duty.

Of the substitute players, only Billy Maharg ever appeared in another major league game. Four years later, he played another one-day stand as an outfielder for the Philadelphia Phillies.

15

Connie Mack's Big Gamble

In 1929 Howard Ehmke of the Philadelphia Athletics was thirty-five years old and in the shadows of a substantial career as a big league pitcher. He had won 166 games and pitched in more than 400 games for Detroit, Boston and Philadelphia in the American League during a career of thirteen seasons. Ehmke had a hunch that his playing days were about to come to an end when Manager Connie Mack called him into his office one morning.

The Philadelphia team was preparing to leave on its last Western trip of the season. They were in first place and running strong. But Mr. Mack told Ehmke that morning that he could pass up no chance to keep his team at top strength. He needed a place on the roster for a young pitcher. And to make room, Howard would have to go.

Ehmke understood the problem. He had pitched in only eleven games all season and knew that he could not take much credit for the Athletic's fine performance. It was likely that a younger man could do more for the team. But Ehmke had one favor to ask.

"I've always wanted to pitch in a World Series," he told Mr. Mack. "And if this is going to be my last season, I'd like to work in this one, if only for a couple of innings. I think I've got one more good game left in this arm of mine."

Mr. Mack studied the old pitcher. The Chicago Cubs were leading the National League by a good margin and would probably be the Athletics' rivals in the World Series. While the Athletics were going West, the Cubs were coming East for series with the Phillies and the Giants.

"All right, Howard," Mr. Mack said. "While we're out West, you follow the Cubs. Watch them play the Phillies and the Giants. See what they like to hit and what their weaknesses are. Don't let anybody know what you're doing. When the World Series comes up, we're going to give everybody a big surprise."

Both the Athletics and the Cubs held their leads and won their pennants as expected. The World Series opened in Chicago on October 8, and it was assumed that Mr. Mack would start one of his pitching aces, George Earnshaw, who had won 24 games that season, Lefty Grove, who had won 20, or Rube Walberg, who had won 18. Even the Philadelphia players were surprised when Howard Ehmke, the fading veteran, began to take his warm-up pitches in front of their dugout before the game.

Ehmke had pitched only fifty-five innings and won only seven games during the season. Everybody in baseball thought he was through. Yet, Mr. Mack dared to start him against one of the hardest-hitting

onnie Mack knew baseball talent and gave Ehmke a last chance for glory.

teams that had ever come into a World Series. The
Chicago line-up included hitters such as Rogers
Hornsby, who had won the National League batting
crown with an average of .380 and was voted the
League's Most Valuable Player; Hack Wilson, who
batted in 159 runs during the season and had a .345
average; Riggs Stephenson, who hit .362; and Kiki
Cuyler, who ended the season at .360.

Mr. Mack was gambling with Ehmke but he knew
baseball talent and believed that the veteran could
win the game. Besides, if Ehmke did lose, the
Athletics still had the rest of their fine pitching staff
in reserve.

Ehmke retired the Cubs in order in the first inning
and finished off the second by striking out Stephenson
and Cuyler.

With one man out in the third inning, the Cubs'
Norman McMillan singled and the next batter, Woody
English, doubled. Now the Cubs had runners on
second and third with only one out. Rogers Hornsby
and Hack Wilson were next in the batting order.
Between them, Hornsby and Wilson had hit seventy-
nine home runs during the season.

Now Ehmke's scouting efforts produced results.
Pitching carefully to their weaknesses, he struck out
both Hornsby and Wilson and brought the third
inning to a stirring close.

Ehmke reached his peak in the sixth inning. There was still no score and the heart of the Chicago batting order was coming up again: English, Hornsby and Wilson.

Ehmke struck out all three of them, and as they went down, the Chicago spirit went down with them.

But the game was still not won. Although Ehmke was holding off the Cubs, the Athletics weren't having any success against the Chicago pitcher, Charlie Root. Finally, in the seventh inning, Jimmy Foxx, the Athletics' powerful first baseman, lifted a home run into the centerfield bleachers to give Ehmke a 1–0 lead.

The Athletics gave Ehmke two more runs in the ninth inning when right fielder Bing Miller singled with men on second and third. Going into the last of the ninth, Philadelphia was ahead, 3–0.

The Cubs threatened in their last time at bat, with the help of an error by the A's third baseman, Jimmy Dykes. With one out, Kiki Cuyler made it to second base when Dykes fumbled a grounder and then threw wild to first base. The next batter singled and Cuyler came home, making the score 3–1.

First baseman Charley Grimm followed with another single. With one out and the tying run on first base, the Cubs sent up two pinch hitters in a row. But Ehmke rose to the occasion once again and retired them both. He completed his great performance by

striking out the last batter, Charlie Tolson, with runners on first and third.

It was Ehmke's thirteenth strikeout of the game. The pitcher that Connie Mack almost released before the season was over not only beat the Cubs, but he also set a World Series record for strikeouts in one game. Although he never won another major league game, Howard Ehmke had proved that there was "one more good game left in this arm of mine."

...hmke justified Mr. Mack's gamble by beating one of the hardest-hitting ...ams ever fielded in a World Series.

16

Opening the Door to Hollywood

A tall, blond young man with a lean frame and a long jaw burst through the door of Branch Rickey's office. Without the usual show of respect, he stalked directly to the old gentleman's desk. The young man leaned over, anger written on his face, and said:

"Don't say a word, Mr. Rickey. This is one conversation I'm conducting."

And in the next ten minutes, Chuck Connors almost talked himself out of the biggest break he would ever get.

The year was 1950. Rickey was then general manager of the Brooklyn Dodgers. The scene was Vero Beach, Florida, where the Dodgers were in spring training. Connors was a first baseman who had been a member of the Dodger organization since 1942.

Before signing with the Dodgers, Connors had attended Seton Hall College where he excelled in public speaking as well as sports. Not only was he a baseball player, but he had done well enough in basketball at Seton Hall to get a chance with the Boston Celtics of the National Basketball Association. However, baseball was his game, and he had moved up gradually through the farm system to the Dodgers.

He was getting his second chance with the Dodgers in 1950 when he confronted Rickey. Connors was known as quite a "ham" among the ballplayers, and he was strictly on-stage with Rickey. His speech was

Chuck practices his slide during spring training at the Dodger camp in 1949.

well-planned, complete with dramatic gestures and dramatic pauses.

Connors reminded Rickey that he had been a star at Montreal the year before, batting .319. Such a performance entitled him to a chance to play regularly with the Dodgers, he said. His conclusion may have been intended as a threat. He told Rickey that if he weren't given a chance with the Dodgers, he wanted to be traded to a team where he could play regularly.

Rickey did not interrupt the rookie's intense presentation. He had known of Connors chiefly through his clubhouse antics. Connors had kept his teammates entertained with his renditions of "Casey at the Bat" and his tricks of magic. He had a flexible face and mimicry came easy for him. One night in a camp show at Vero Beach, Connors had gained the spotlight with an imitation of Rickey himself, picturing Rickey as a merciless penny pincher and the Dodger camp as a prison.

Although Connors had tried everything to get a chance at first base, Manager Shotton had persistently stuck to Gil Hodges and Dee Fondy. Occasionally he would call on Connors, but usually he appeared only in "B" squad games. Rickey may have recalled, as he watched Connors' dramatics, that Connors had been to bat only once in the National League and had hit into a double play.

"My boy," said Rickey, as Connors finished, "you are absolutely right. You deserve the chance to play more often. I'll give it to you right now."

In the time that it takes to place a long distance telephone call, Rickey sold Connors to the St. Louis Browns. Connors was crestfallen. This was worse than being in Montreal, because the Browns were the worst club in the American League. Besides, they paid even lower salaries than the Dodgers.

Two hours later, after he had wandered about the camp thinking about what he had done, Connors was back at Rickey's door again.

"Call it off, Mr. Rickey, please," he said. "I'll go to Montreal, if you promise to trade me to another National League club at the end of the season."

Rickey agreed, and at the end of the season Connors was sold to the Chicago Cubs. Even with this lowly member of the National League he couldn't break into the line-up. Shortly afterward he found himself playing on option in Los Angeles with a Pacific Coast League team. To add to his discouragement, Connors had been beaten out in Chicago by one of his Brooklyn teammates who had also been traded to the Cubs, Dee Fondy.

It was a despondent Connors who reported to Los Angeles at the beginning of the 1951 season. What he didn't know was that he was walking into an opportunity that would completely reshape his life.

Movie figures are devoted baseball fans in Los Angeles. They were attracted to Connors, who had now carried his antics to the playing field. He was also hitting home runs with impressive regularity, and this made him even more noticeable.

In fact, his fine performance even brought about the one big baseball break he had been playing for. At midseason, he had a batting average of .321, with 22 home runs and 77 runs batted in, and the Cubs recalled him.

Connors finished the season in Chicago, but he was a big disappointment to himself and to the Cubs. After batting only .239 in 66 games, he was returned to Los Angeles for the 1952 season. He increased his mischievousness on the field. "If I'm not going to make it in the big leagues," he told a teammate, "I might as well have some fun out of life."

One night Connors hit a home run, and as he neared second on his way around the bases, he suddenly slid into the bag in a cloud of dust, and arose making a sweeping bow. When he reached the plate, he stopped and vigorously shook the hand of the opposing catcher, then hammed it up all the way back to the dugout.

After the game, there was a call for Connors at the Angels' dressing room: a man named Grady from MGM. Connors was somewhat suspicious, but went out to meet the man anyway. The caller was Bill

Grady, a casting director from Metro–Goldwyn–Mayer, one of Hollywood's biggest movie studios. He offered Connors the chance to make $500 a day as an actor. Connors could hardly believe his ears.

As it turned out, Chuck didn't get the part that Grady had picked him for, a prize-fight tough. Connors just couldn't look battered enough or dumb enough for the role. But he did get the part of a clean-cut state patrolman.

After receiving his check for $500, he called Bill Grady. "Any more jobs like that around?" Chuck asked.

"Not right now," Grady told him, "but I'll keep you in mind."

Shortly afterward Connors did get a call from Grady. "I've got a part for you in 'South Seas Woman,'" he said.

This paid $750 a week, and the job lasted thirteen weeks. Altogether during that winter, Chuck made $15,000 as a movie actor. He had made only $6,500 in his eighth season as a baseball player the previous summer.

When Connors' baseball contract arrived, it was another invitation to join the Cubs. He had developed a big following among Los Angeles fans and the Cubs wanted him back. Despite this second chance with the Chicago team, baseball had become less important to Connors. He decided to quit baseball altogether. Chuck Connors, first baseman, became Chuck Connors, actor.

His reputation grew rapidly in Hollywood. He received many movie parts, usually in Westerns. Then, television called and his audience grew. He played the title role in the "The Rifleman" series. Next, he starred in "Branded" and then organized his own production company.

Although his career as a first baseman never worked out the way he planned it, Chuck never failed to be grateful to baseball for opening the door to Hollywood.

In his first season as an actor Chuck Connors earned more than twice his salary as a baseball player. He is seen here as the hero of the TV show "Branded."

17
The Shoeshine Pitch

The fourth game of the 1957 World Series is described by many baseball observers as one of the most exciting in history. Had it not been for Vernal "Nippy" Jones, it might not have been.

The Milwaukee Braves were playing their first World Series since the team had been moved from Boston. The Series had opened in New York, where the Braves lost the first game to the Yankees and won the second.

Wisconsin was bursting with excitement when the two teams moved to Milwaukee for the next three games. It was the first time a World Series had ever been played in Wisconsin. Some of the enthusiasm faded, however, when the Braves' pitchers walked eleven Yankees and lost the first home game, 12–3.

Going into the fourth game, the Braves were trailing, two games to one. Warren Spahn, the greatest left-handed pitcher in baseball, was chosen to pitch against the Yankees. The appearance of their pitching star restored confidence to the anxious Milwaukeeans.

After eight innings, the crafty veteran led the Yankees by a score of 4–1. He retired the first two batters in the ninth, but then Yogi Berra, the squat Yankee catcher, singled. So did the next batter, Gil McDougald.

Apprehension spread among loyal Braves fans, but

115

With a 3 and 2 count on Elston Howard, Spahn gave up a three-run homer which tied the fourth game of the 1957 Series.

many thousands of them who had made an early start to the parking lot kept moving. Surely Spahn would not let them down this close to victory. A conference was held on the mound. Manager Fred Haney was confident, too, that Spahn would not let the Braves down. He offered a few words of encouragement and went back to the dugout, leaving the crisis in Spahn's care.

Elston Howard was the next Yankee at bat. He was a dangerous right-handed hitter. Spahn worked carefully and the count reached 3 and 2.

"This is it," said the radio announcer. "The Yankees trail 4–1 in the top of the ninth. There are two out and two men on. The count on Elston Howard is three balls, two strikes. . . .

"Spahn sets, checks both runners and delivers. Howard swings and he gets hold of one . . . It's a long fly . . . it's going, going . . ."

There was no doubt about it—it was a home run. With one swing of the bat, Elston Howard had tied the game. In the parking lot, there was confusion. Milwaukee fans gulped. Many rushed back to their seats in the stadium. Others tuned in the game on their automobile radios and hoped. This couldn't happen, they thought. The Yankees couldn't win. If they beat Spahn, the Braves' ace, the World Series was lost.

Milwaukee failed to score in the ninth, and the tenth began on an ominous note. Tony Kubek of the Yankees, a native Milwaukeean, beat out an infield roller. Hank Bauer then hit a triple that scored Kubek and put New York in the lead, 5–4.

Defeat seemed certain as the Braves came to bat in the tenth inning. There was little cause for rejoicing when it was announced that number 25, Nippy Jones, would bat for Spahn.

Jones was what is known in professional baseball

as a "retread," meaning that he had played in the major leagues and then had been sent back to the minors. He had been the regular first baseman for the Cardinals at one time and later played for the Phillies. An injury to his back followed by a serious operation brought an end to his usefulness as a day-by-day player and his release to the minors.

When Joe Adcock, the Braves' star first baseman, suffered a broken leg in midseason, Jones was hastily brought up to Milwaukee from Sacramento, a Pacific Coast League team. Jones had been used chiefly as a relief player during the season, filling in at first base on occasion, and pinch-hitting.

Now he walked to the plate, a slight, somber man with dark, sad eyes. He tapped the dirt from his spikes, and faced Tommy Byrne, a Yankee relief pitcher known for his wildness.

Byrne's first pitch was low. The ball got away from catcher Yogi Berra and skittered back to the grandstand wall. Jones started toward first base, but was called back by umpire Augie Donatelli. A fierce argument broke out. Jones argued that the pitch had hit his foot. Donatelli said the pitch was a ball and ordered Jones back into the batter's box.

As the argument raged, the ball rolled back on the rebound from the cement wall, coming to rest between Jones and Donatelli. The crowd saw Jones reach

Ump Augie Donatelli shows game-winning shoe polish to catcher Yogi Berra while Nippy Jones points to his shoes. The Braves went on to win the Series in seven games.

suddenly for the ball, then thrust it in the face of Donatelli.

"Here!" Jones cried, "Look at the shoe polish on the ball!"

There was a black splotch on the baseball, and as Jones pointed first to the ball, then to his brightly shined shoes, Donatelli was convinced. The Milwaukee pinch hitter was awarded first base. He was immediately replaced by a pinch runner. He retired to the dugout and did not appear again in the series.

But this insignificant incident seemed to set the Braves on fire. Their shortstop, Johnny Logan, slashed a double into left field, scoring the pinch runner and tying the game. Casey Stengel came out to change pitchers and the Milwaukee fans jeered the crusty old Yankee manager.

Ed Mathews, the Braves' power-hitting third baseman, came up to face the new pitcher, Bob Grim. Mathews looked at a couple of pitches, then swung on a fast ball and drove a home run into the right center field bleachers, scoring Logan ahead of him, and winning the game, 7–5.

Milwaukee went wild that night. The fans had seen the Yankees beaten and the Series tied at two games apiece. Encouraged by their victory, the Braves rode on to triumph in seven games. Lou Burdette, a rawboned, right-handed pitcher, won three games, and Henry Aaron, the center fielder, was the batting leader.

But the great Braves victory might never have happened if it hadn't been for Nippy Jones, who kept his shoes well shined.

18
Back Road to the Hall of Fame

Dazzy Vance was never sure what happened to his pitching arm early in his career. He thought he injured it for the first time boxing with one of his brothers before he left his home near Red Cloud, Nebraska, for spring training in 1916. He was hoping to join the New York Yankees, for whom he had pitched in nine games the season before without a victory.

He was sent to the minors for the 1916 season and for the next five years his pitching career was hampered by his sore arm. Managers began to squint at him suspiciously and ask, "Vance, do you really *want* to pitch, or not?"

Sometimes Vance felt like telling them the truth. His arm often hurt so badly that he really *didn't* want to pitch. But he had a family to support and baseball was the only business he knew.

Once, when he was pitching for Columbus, Ohio, he stuck his elbow in ice water between innings to numb the pain. This worked for a couple of games. Finally even the ice water did no good, and the Columbus club sent him home to see a doctor in Nebraska.

"I can't tell you exactly what the trouble is," the doctor told Vance, "but I believe that if you can keep from hurting it again in the next four or five years, it'll come around all right."

"Four to five years, Doc!" Vance exclaimed. "And how am I going to eat in the meantime?"

In the spring of 1917 Vance was back in training, this time with the Toledo, Ohio, team. He looked great in exhibitions, but as the season opened he began to tire easily and the opposition started to slaughter him. He moved on to Memphis but the same thing happened. At first Vance dazzled batters with his fiery fast ball, but then he would tire and have to leave the game. He was called up to the New York Yankees again in 1918. But he pitched only two games before returning to the minors.

This was the pattern of Dazzy Vance's life until 1920, when he found himself in Memphis. The manager of the Memphis team was a grumpy veteran named Spencer Abbott. Short of patience and firmly convinced that Vance was too lazy or too yellow to pitch, he traded the tall right-hander to New Orleans.

Soon Vance's arm was beginning to feel good again. About two weeks after being traded to New Orleans, Vance beat Memphis with a terrific performance. Abbott was angry. "Why didn't you pitch that way for me?" he said to Vance, meeting him in the hotel doorway that night.

"I kept trying to tell you," Vance said. "I didn't have my strength yet, and I needed plenty of rest. They're giving me rest at New Orleans, and I'm winning."

Vance kept on winning. The next season at New Orleans—1921—he won twenty-one games. This attracted the attention of the Brooklyn Dodgers, but only by accident.

New Orleans had a catcher named Hank DeBerry who was making a name for himself in the Southern Association. Wilbert Robinson, manager of the Dodgers, needed a catcher badly and sent his top scout, Larry Sutton, to take a look at DeBarry.

Returning to Brooklyn, Sutton told Robinson, "We not only need DeBerry, but they've got a pitcher we ought to get, too. His name is Vance."

By this time Vance was thirty-one years old, though nobody but his family knew it. He had played with twelve different teams in every kind of town, and his sore arm was well-known. Nevertheless, Sutton insisted that Robinson buy him. And Vance became a Dodger.

Not many people were optimistic about Vance's chance of staying with the National League team. Even Vance wondered if he could make it. But, one day in Mobile, Alabama, the Dodgers stopped to play the St. Louis Browns in a spring exhibition game. George Sisler, one of the great hitters of all time, came to bat against Vance. The 31-year-old rookie reared back in a big sweeping motion until his arm almost touched the ground, then delivered the ball with a big kick of the foot. It was a strike.

With two strikes on Sisler, Vance broke off a big curve that caught the great hitter with his bat on the shoulder. Sisler knew he was out, and he turned and walked away without a word.

"They told me Vance was strictly a fast-ball pitcher," Robinson said, excitedly. "Look at the way he got Sisler on that curve. Anybody who can catch Sisler looking at a curve must be throwing a pretty good one."

From then on, Vance was established as a Dodger. He won eighteen games during his first season and led the league in strikeouts. He won eighteen games the next year and again led the league in strikeouts. His third season with the Dodgers was his finest. He won twenty-eight games and lost only six. Once again he led the league in strikeouts, and he was voted the most valuable player. Vance led in strikeouts seven years in a row, something no other pitcher has ever done.

His name became synonymous with speed. Little boys playing sandlot ball and fancying themselves as hitters pretended they were Babe Ruth. Sandlot pitchers who tried to throw the ball hard were patterning themselves after Dazzy Vance.

When he retired, Vance had won 197 games and

Dazzy was traded to New Orleans because his manager thought he was too lazy or too yellow to pitch.

had struck out 2,045 batters. He pitched until he was forty-four years old, and in the twilight of his career realized one of his cherished ambitions. In 1934 he made his only appearance in a World Series, pitching in relief for the St. Louis Cardinals against Detroit. He pitched only one and one-third innings, but he was at his dazzling best, shutting out the Tigers and striking out three batters.

Vance's last great thrill came to him many years later, a most improbable climax to a most improbable career. One spring day in 1954, as he drove along a highway near his home in Homosassa Springs, Florida, a state patrolman roared up behind him and motioned him over to the side of the road.

"Hey, what's the big idea?" asked Dazzy as the patrolman approached his car. "Is something wrong?"

"Not a thing, Mr. Vance," said the patrolman. "Everything's fine, in fact. I just stopped you to tell you that you've been voted into the Hall of Fame."

What are the odds against a pitcher who didn't win his first game in the major leagues until he was thirty-one years old ever making the Baseball Hall of Fame? Maybe 1,000,000 to 1. But Dazzy Vance made it and he did it the hard way, sore arm and all.

a Dodger, Vance became a sandlot idol. His name was synonymous
th a blazing fastball.

19

Lt. Shepard of the Big Leagues

One day in early March, 1945, a young man named Bert Shepard appeared at the preseason training camp of the Washington Senators at College Park, Maryland, and sought out Manager Ossie Bluege.

"I'd like to get a tryout, Mr. Bluege," the young man said.

Bluege, a man with cold, steel-blue eyes, looked the applicant up and down. "What experience have you had?" he asked.

Shepard explained that he had played in the Wisconsin State League, the Evangeline League and the Arizona-Texas League. During the war, he said, he had pitched and played first base for service teams.

The United States was still at war with the Germans and the Japanese. Baseball players were becoming more scarce each day, since nearly all able-bodied men were in the armed forces. No sensible manager would turn down any likely applicant, especially one who looked as healthy and athletic as this one. Bluege took Shepard to the clubhouse and asked the trainer to find a uniform for him.

The day's workout hadn't yet begun. A few Washington players still loitered in the clubhouse as Shepard began to change from street clothes into the flannel uniform. At first, the other players didn't take much notice of him. In those times they were accustomed to seeing players walk in off the street, ask for a tryout and just as suddenly disappear.

But as Bert Shepard switched trousers, it was easy to see that he had an artificial leg. He was a one-legged player.

When he walked onto the field his limp was noticeable, but only because the other players now knew of his handicap. They were amazed and touched to see a one-legged man who insisted he could play professional baseball. He soon proved that he could.

Being a professional baseball player was Bert Shepard's big ambition when he enlisted in the Army in 1942. Now the war was over for him but his ambition was still the same.

The baseball season was supposed to begin for the 55th Fighter Group team, based in England, on May 21, 1944. Lieutenant Bert Shepard was the manager as well as the star pitcher. First, though, there was a mission to be flown over Germany.

Early that morning, Lieutenant Shepard and a flight of P-38 fighter planes set out for the target in Germany. By this time Shepard was a veteran. He had flown thirty-three missions, and he felt that he was the master of the sky.

The game was scheduled for 2 P.M. There was plenty of time to complete the mission and get back to play, he thought, as he flew over the North Sea toward the target at 300 miles per hour.

The attacking force had completed its run on the target and was preparing to head back to base when Shepard spotted a train chugging along below. One purpose of the mission was to strafe anything that moved, and Lieutenant Shepard put his P-38 into a dive toward the train. The train was in smoke and flames, and he was about to pull up when ground fire struck the cockpit. He tried desperately to pull out of range, but then another burst of fire hit him. That is the last he remembered.

Several days later, he awoke in a German prison hospital and discovered that his right leg was missing, amputated just below the knee. It had been mangled by antiaircraft fire, and the German doctors had hurriedly removed it. They had done a good job, but what use is a one-legged baseball player?

The longer he lay in bed, however, the more determined he became that he should be a baseball player, even with only one leg. Meanwhile, back at the 55th Fighter Group base in England, the boys on the baseball team finally gave up hope for their manager after two weeks.

Shepard had been in the Washington Senators' camp only five days when newsreel cameramen appeared to make movies of this unusual baseball player.

It would be great for the soldiers' morale.

"Can you field bunts?" one of them asked.

Shepard had been wearing his artificial leg only one week. It had been attached the day before he left nearby Walter Reed Hospital. But he was game. "Sure, I can field bunts," he said. "Let me know when you're ready."

Al Evans stepped up to bat. Shepard pitched and Evans laid the ball down between the mound and third base. Shepard swooped down on it, wheeled as a left-handed pitcher must and threw Evans out by a step.

On April first, the Senators traveled to Norfolk, Virginia, to play the Naval Training base team. With a comfortable lead in the eighth inning, Bluege decided to test the one-legged pitcher and Shepard marched to the mound with 8,000 servicemen looking on.

The first batter immediately laid down a bunt. Shepard whipped off the mound, pounced on the ball and threw the runner out easily, while servicemen cheered in approval. The next batter grounded out to first and the second hit a fly to center field.

That was enough. Shepard had proved he could pitch, run and even pinch-hit, if necessary. Clark Griffith, the white-haired owner of the Senators, signed him to a contract. There was never a happier

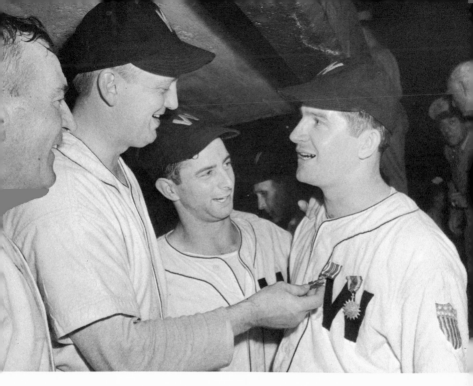

Teammates admire the Distinguished Flying Cross awarded to Shepard during a colorful homeplate ceremony.

man than Bert Shepard.

The first few weeks of the 1945 season weren't easy for him. He wanted to pitch, but Bluege used him mostly for batting practice, and Griffith used him mostly as a display to other handicapped servicemen who might be feeling sorry for themselves. Frequently Shepard went back to his old ward at Walter Reed Hospital to cheer up his wounded comrades.

Finally, one day in July, he got his first real chance. The Senators were scheduled to play the Brooklyn Dodgers in a war-relief exhibition game.

Bluege asked Shepard if he thought he could beat

them. Shepard, knowing that this was his first chance against major league competition, said he thought he could. Bluege started him in the exhibition. Shepard pitched against the Dodgers and was credited with the victory.

Late in July, the Senators were playing Boston and found themselves several runs behind early in the game. Bluege saw that he would need a relief pitcher to start the next inning and told Shepard to warm up. But the Red Sox kept up a steady bombardment and finally Bluege had to come out of the dugout.

After a conference with the pitcher, he motioned for Shepard. The former fighter pilot, walking with that slight trace of a limp, moved from the bull pen to the pitcher's mound. Everybody knew of him by now, and his performance was watched intently.

Shepard retired the last man of the inning. Then he went one, two, three innings. Finally the Red Sox got a run, but he finished the fifth relief inning and the game. Boston had managed to get only three hits and one run in the five innings and he had struck out three batters.

Shepard's career was a short one. His leg was bothering him. He had to return to Walter Reed Hospital for adjustments of the artificial limb. Afterward, the Senators sent him to their Chattanooga farm

Even with a wooden leg, Bert could pitch, run and hit. Here he warms up for the Washington Senators.

team, where he won two games and lost two games.

"I'll be back," he said when he left.

He did return to the Senators, but they never used him in another regular season game. Still, he had kept the vow he made in a hospital bed in Germany. Bert Shepard had become a major league pitcher, if only for a day.

20

The Tag-Along

When they were kids in Phoenix, Arizona, Ted Smith wanted to be a big league baseball player and Gordon Windhorn dreamed of nothing but being a track star. Whenever there was a baseball game in the neighborhood, Ted would show up with his glove in his hand. Gordon was a good runner and concentrated on making his high-school track team.

One day a notice appeared in a Phoenix newspaper that the New York Giants would conduct a baseball tryout in the city. Ted had played sandlot baseball and his coaches had told him he was a good outfielder. A tryout with the New York Giants, he felt, was his big chance.

There was just one drawback. Ted was shy and didn't want to go alone. Gordon Windhorn was his good friend, so Ted decided to ask him to go to the tryouts. Gordon had played baseball only a few times. When Ted asked him to go along, he protested that he didn't even have any equipment. Ted offered to borrow some for him and Gordon reluctantly agreed to go.

The next afternoon, Ted went to the Windhorn home carrying a baseball uniform, a glove and spikes for Gordon and a set of equipment for himself. Arriving at the ball park, the two boys were sent to a locker room to dress.

"I feel silly, putting this thing on," Gordon said,

buttoning his baseball shirt. "I'm a runner, not a baseball player."

"Baseball players have to run, too," Ted said. "Tell them you're an outfielder. All they'll do is hit fly balls to you and you can catch them easily."

Despite Ted's assurances, Gordon was afraid of making a fool of himself. Out on the field, he took his glove and eased toward the outfield, hoping nobody would notice him.

"Hey, boy!" shouted a uniformed man with a bat. "Get this one!"

The man lofted a fly over Gordon's head. Gordon turned in two directions, then set out on a run. He stuck out his glove and the ball hit it with a plop— a perfect catch! The man hit another, and once again Gordon managed to get under the ball and catch it. There was something lacking in his style, but with great bursts of speed he always managed to get to the ball.

A little later, Gordon was called in to the dugout. "You're the kid that was making all those catches out there, aren't you?" said the man in charge. "Now let's see what you can do with a bat."

Gordon said, "Okay, mister, I'll try." He had played softball a few times and he knew at least how to swing a bat.

Gordon rifled the first pitch to left field for a clean

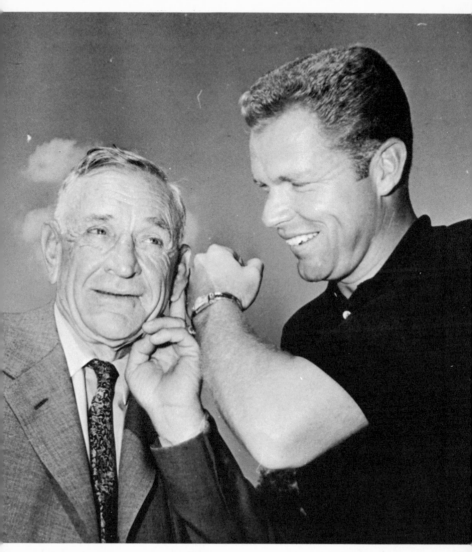

Outfielder Windhorn shows Yankee manager Casey Stengel the wrist watch awarded to him as outstanding Yankee rookie.

hit. He hit the next one so hard that Ted, who had been moved in to shortstop, couldn't handle it. This impressive exhibition continued through five more pitches, after which Gordon was allowed to return to the outfield.

When the tryout was over that afternoon, the uniformed man called all the players around him. He picked out five and asked them to step to one side. One of them was Gordon Windhorn.

"How would you boys like to play for the New York Giants?" he said. "If you would, I've got contracts here for all of you."

In the crowd of players who didn't make it, Gordon could see the crestfallen face of his friend, Ted Smith. He could hardly force himself to look at Ted as they walked home.

"Honest, Ted, I never had any idea I could play baseball," he said. "I'm awful sorry."

"Sorry?" Ted said. "It's great. It won't be long. I'll make it sometime, too, and we'll play in the big leagues together."

But Ted never made it. He finally gave up the game and found a job in Phoenix. Gordon Windhorn was never a big star, but he did play for the Red Sox, the Yankees, the Kansas City Athletics and the Los Angeles Dodgers. He is one of the few who became a major league player by accident.

Playing for the Los Angeles Dodgers, Windhorn slams into the wall in an effort to catch a long fly.

21
Young Man in a Hurry

Ty Cobb's father was a stern man who took a dim view of his son's interest in professional baseball. He was a superintendent of schools in Royston, Georgia, and he regarded baseball as a game for boys and men who were too lazy to get a steady job. But since his son was determined to try out for the minor league team in Augusta, Georgia, Mr. Cobb thought it best to let young Ty get baseball out of his system. He gave Ty 90 dollars and several letters of introduction to people who might help him if his baseball career didn't work out. Then he sent him on his way.

Two days after the baseball season opened in Augusta, Ty, who was only seventeen years old, suddenly found himself out of work. The manager of the Augusta team, a grumpy man named Con Strouthers, called him in and gave him his release.

Another player, released at the same time, had an offer from a semiprofessional team in Anniston, Alabama, and invited Cobb to join him. Ty wanted to go along but decided to call his father first. It was a nervous young man who telephoned from Augusta to Royston that night, explaining to his father that he had been released from the Augusta team and asking permission to try his luck in Alabama. There was a long pause while the static cracked over the telephone lines. Then Mr. Cobb spoke. "Go after it," he said, "and don't come home a failure."

The Anniston team was made up mostly of young collegians and a few wandering ex-professionals. The club paid Cobb 65 dollars a month, plus room and board in a private home. After Augusta, making the Anniston team was easy. Soon, Cobb became one of the best hitters in the league. But since this was a semiprofessional league, little news of his success got beyond the local papers. None of it got as far as the Atlanta *Journal,* which his father subscribed to and read every day.

One day, Grantland Rice, the popular young sports editor of the *Journal,* received a post card from Anniston, telling him about the splendid young outfielder named Cobb:

Ty Cobb, dashing young star with Anniston, Alabama, is going great guns. He is as fast as a deer and undoubtedly a phenom.

(Signed) Mr. Jones

Soon another card reached Rice's desk. It said:

Cobb had three hits yesterday, made two sensational catches. Keep your eye on this phenom.
(Signed) Smith, Brown, Kelly and McIntyre

More cards and letters arrived, all recommending this superb young outfielder from Anniston:

ung Ty Cobb was hardly modest but who could object? He had a tting average of .370!

If you're searching for a future star, he's playing here in Anniston. His name is Cobb. He's a Georgia boy who's going a long way.

(Signed) Interested Fan

This is the one that aroused Rice's writing interest. Since this fantastic lad with the enthusiastic backing was a Georgia boy, he should be mentioned in Rice's column.

He finally wrote one day, "Rumors have reached Atlanta from numerous sources that over in Alabama there's a young fellow named Cobb who seems to be showing an unusual lot of talent for baseball. Furthermore, he's a Georgian."

Back in Royston, Mr. Cobb clipped the little article out of the *Journal* and carried it in his wallet as proof that his son had made good. And in Augusta, the article encouraged the baseball team to do some checking. It soon learned that the slender young man who had been hastily dismissed was batting .370 in Anniston. He was soon brought back and restored to the line-up.

There was no slowing Cobb's drive to the top now. He finished the 1904 season with Augusta and was called to the Detroit Tigers before the next season was over. There he became one of the truly great baseball players. He never did get baseball out of

It was many years before sports writer Grantland Rice learned who had written all those glowing reports on Cobb.

his system as his father had hoped. He played for twenty-four years in the major leagues. After his first season, he never batted below .300 and he led the American League in batting eleven times. Three times he batted over .400. In addition, he stole 892 bases. Years later, he was one of the first five men voted into the Baseball Hall of Fame. He received more votes than Babe Ruth or Christy Mathewson.

Many years later, Cobb happened to be seated next to Grantland Rice on the speaker's platform at a sports banquet. Cobb was nearing the end of his great playing career with Detroit and Rice had been successful, too; he had become the most famous sports writer in America.

The speakers were reminiscing about great past sports events and when Cobb's turn came, he spoke to Rice. "Grant," he began, "you remember when you were sports editor of the Atlanta *Journal,* and I was just starting out in baseball?"

"You bet I remember," Rice said. "I first heard of you when you were playing for a team in Anniston, Alabama."

"And do you remember all the cards and letters you used to get from the fans in Anniston, telling you what a great prospect I was?" Cobb asked.

"They swamped me," Rice said. "In fact, they wrote you right out of Anniston back to Augusta."

"I was playing pretty well," Cobb said, "but I must have been a pretty good writer, too, because I wrote those cards and letters myself."

Rice was silent for a moment. The joke was certainly on him. But then his face broke into a big smile. He reached out and shook Cobb's hand, and they both understood.

Cobb would have succeeded in baseball sooner or later. He had too much talent to be ignored for long. But even when he was only seventeen, he had a tremendous desire to succeed—he had been a young man in a big hurry.

22
Two for the Price of One

A crowd of only 3,500 came out to Weeghman Park in Chicago on the afternoon of May 2, 1917. Weeghman Park, the home of the Chicago Cubs, was later renamed Wrigley Field. It was a weekday, accounting for the light attendance, and the Cubs were playing the Cincinnati Reds. If Cub fans had known what was going to happen they would have come in greater numbers.

Jim "Hippo" Vaughn, a big left-handed pitcher from Texas, was starting for the Cubs against Cincinnati's Fred Toney, a right-hander from Tennessee. Both pitchers were on their way to splendid seasons, Toney to win 24 games and Vaughn to win 23.

Something extra rode on the game because Toney and Vaughn were not particularly friendly. Vaughn came from a tough breed of players who felt that even to speak to a member of another team on the field violated an unwritten code.

The first inning began with two Cincinnati batters going down in rapid order. The third Red, outfielder Earle "Greasy" Neale (he was later head football coach of the Philadelphia Eagles) hit a soft line drive that looked like a hit. But the Cubs' right fielder, Cy Williams, put on a burst of speed coming in for the ball, and made the catch at his shoetops. Otherwise, the game moved along without any threat of a hit for several innings.

153

Reds Manager Pat Moran had stacked the Cincinnati line-up with right-handed hitters, since the averages said that right-handers would be more likely to hit Vaughn's left-handed pitching. This had been no handicap to Vaughn, however. He had been mowing down the Reds with regularity.

After he had set down Cincinnati in the eighth inning, Vaughn reached the bench in time to hear a teammate say, "Come on, fellows, let's get a run off this guy!"

"Get a run?" said another Cub. "Somebody better think about getting a hit first."

"Well," said the first teammate, "they haven't got a hit off Hippo yet, either."

Suddenly Vaughn realized that both he and Toney had no-hit games within their reach. As he silently pulled on his sweater to keep his arm warm between innings, Vaughn thought to himself, "Well, if this is a no-hitter and there's only one more inning to go, I'm going to give it all I've got."

Once again in the last of the eighth the Cubs went up to bat and down in one–two–three order, and Vaughn headed back to the mound for the ninth inning. The first man up hit a line drive to the Cub third baseman. Vaughn threw three strikes past Emil Huhn, the weak-hitting Cincinnati catcher.

That brought up Toney, a big man and a dangerous

hitter for a pitcher. He had a powerful stiff-armed swing, and on Vaughn's first pitch he swung fiercely and missed. Two more pitches, each a fast ball, put Toney out on strikes to end the inning, but it was a tired Vaughn who returned to the Chicago dugout.

In the last of the ninth Toney set down the Cubs in order again. This was enough for historical purposes. Both pitchers had pitched complete no-hit games against one another, the only time it has ever happened in the major leagues.

But the game still had to be won. The small crowd sounded like 10,000 as they cheered Vaughn on his weary way back to the mound to face the Reds in the first half of the tenth inning.

Gus Getz, the first Red to bat, popped out to catcher Art Wilson. The next batter, shortstop Larry Kopf, was only a .255 batter, but he broke the spell. He slapped a ground ball between the first and second baseman into right field for the first hit of the game. Vaughn then retired Neale on a fly ball to Williams, and it looked as though he was out of trouble, even though his no-hitter was gone.

But then misfortune fell on the Cubs. Hal Chase, the Cincinnati first baseman, hit a sinking line drive to center field. Williams reached the ball in time for the catch—but he dropped it for an error. Now Kopf was on third, Chase was on first, and Indian Jim

Thorpe was at bat.

Although Thorpe excelled as a college football player and as an Olympic track star, he never mastered baseball. He was swift as a deer and had a strong arm, but his downfall was the curve ball. He could hit a fast ball out of the park, but throw him a curve and he was helpless. Jim had already struck out twice that afternoon on Vaughn's curve.

As Vaughn delivered his first pitch, Chase broke for second and slid in with a clean steal. Vaughn worked very carefully on Thorpe. With two runners in scoring position, naturally he called on his curve and Thorpe swung, topping the ball and sending it spinning down the third baseline.

Big Vaughn leaped from the mound and fielded the ball, but too late to make a play for the speedy Thorpe at first. Had he not had his back to Kopf, he could have turned and tagged the Cincinnati shortstop. But Kopf sped by him and headed for the plate.

There was still time to get Kopf at home, and Vaughn threw to Wilson, the catcher. For some reason, Wilson was looking toward first base, apparently expecting the play there. The ball hit his chest protector and dropped to the ground while Kopf slid under him. Now Chase was also on his way toward the plate. Wilson, coming out of his stupor, scrambled for the third out.

The damage was done, though. The Reds were ahead 1–0 and Toney again retired the Cubs in order in the last of the tenth. The double no-hitter was over, Toney the winner, Vaughn the loser.

In the clubhouse, Wilson was in tears. "I just passed out on you Jim," he said to Vaughn. "I just passed out. It was all my fault."

Vaughn was a good sport, however. "Don't blame yourself, Art," he told his catcher. "It's just another ball game."

It was hardly just another ball game. There has never been one like it in the major leagues. Because of his defeat that day, Jim Vaughn promised himself he would never lose again to Fred Toney. And he never did.

23

The
Iron
Horse

On June 2, 1925, the first baseman for the New York Yankees, a veteran named Wally Pipp, told Manager Miller Huggins that he had a headache and would appreciate the day off. Huggins was sympathetic and decided to give the "new kid" a chance.

The "new kid" was Lou Gehrig who had not yet reached his twenty-second birthday. He had been discovered two years earlier when he was a pitcher and outfielder for Columbia University and had played in only a handful of games for the Yankees. But as Pipp said later, what he got that day wasn't a rest, it was a retirement. Young Gehrig did so well at first base that Pipp never got back into the regular line-up and was sold the next season to Cincinnati.

It was nearly fourteen years before Gehrig gave up his place in the line-up. Starting on June 2, 1925, he played in every Yankee game until May 1, 1939. He appeared in 2,130 consecutive games, a record so amazing that it is likely never to be broken. For his reliability, Gehrig was called "The Iron Horse."

But Gehrig was more than reliable. As a young man of twenty-two, he had earned a place with the New York Yankees, who were then the strongest team in baseball. One of Gehrig's teammates was Babe Ruth, who had already established himself as the "Home Run King." But even though the Yankees were one of the greatest teams in history, Gehrig soon be-

159

Lou, shown here fresh out of Columbia University, was soon to become known as "The Iron Horse."

came one of the greatest of the great.

Two years after he took Wally Pipp's place at first base, Gehrig showed his talent. It was 1927. The Yankees won the pennant by nineteen games and Babe Ruth became a baseball legend by hitting sixty home runs. Meanwhile, Gehrig batted .373 and set another all-time record by batting in 175 runs. When the award to the most valuable player in the league was given, it went not to the famous and colorful Ruth but to Lou Gehrig, who was still in his early twenties.

Gehrig went on to break his own RBI record, batting in 184 runs in 1931, a record that still stands in the American League. He led the league five times in runs batted in, four times in runs scored, three times in home runs and once in batting average. Perhaps more important, he was named the most valuable player in his league four times.

As the season ended in 1938, a few fans and writers wondered if Gehrig was beginning to fade. He had batted only .295, the first time his average had fallen under .300 in thirteen seasons. Although he had hit 29 home runs and batted in 114 runs—a good performance for most players—he was still not as sharp as he had been in previous years.

In the spring of 1939, Gehrig was even less impressive. He seemed to move around rather stiffly and his batting eye was off. Sports writers had reported that he was suffering from lumbago during the previous season and many assumed that it was still plaguing him. During the first eight games, Gehrig could get only four hits, all singles. His batting average was .143. In the field, he was clumsy and slow, although people remembered him as a fine first baseman.

On April 30, the Yankees set out on their first

Lou makes a play at first base.

Western trip of the season. Gehrig had played in the last home game against Washington that afternoon and by the time the team reached Detroit he had reached a great personal decision. He came down from his room in the Book Cadillac Hotel and found the Yankee manager, Joe McCarthy, in the lobby. He asked for a private word with him.

"I think you'd better put Babe Dahlgren in at first base today," Gehrig told McCarthy. "I'm not doing myself or the team any good."

McCarthy tried to talk Lou out of his decision but Gehrig stood firm.

"The other day I made a routine play at first base," he said, "and when I got back to the bench the fellows said 'Nice play, Lou.' When they start feeling sorry for you and it shows, it's time to quit."

McCarthy reluctantly called a press conference and announced that "The Iron Horse" was benching himself. This was more than an ordinary change in the line-up. It was the end of Gehrig's great endurance record.

When Gehrig's withdrawal from the line-up was announced, most people assumed that it would mean only a short rest, because he was only thirty-five. But like Wally Pipp, who had given up his place for a rest fourteen years earlier, Gehrig never appeared again. Two years later, he was dead of a disease known as amyotrophic lateral sclerosis, which had already begun to cripple him when he gave up his job in Detroit.

There was a rare twist to Gehrig's retirement from the line-up. Sitting in the lobby of the Book Cadillac Hotel that day was a gray-haired businessman from Grand Rapids, Michigan. He had come to Detroit to see the Yankees play. His name—Wally Pipp.

24
The Double No-Hit

On the night of June 15, 1938, a crowd of 38,748 people came to Ebbets Field in Brooklyn to see the first baseball game played under lights in New York City. The major attraction was the novelty of night baseball. But a secondary attraction was a 22-year-old, left-handed pitcher for the visiting Cincinnati Reds, Johnny Vander Meer. Five days before the Brooklyn game, Vander Meer had pitched a no-hit game in Cincinnati and had beaten the Boston club, then known as the Bees, 3–0.

Vander Meer was in his first year in the majors and his no-hitter had made him the talk of the town. But while he had blinding speed, he was almost as wild as he was fast. And since he was new in the League, his knowledge of National League batters was limited. Some said his no-hitter was a fluke.

Johnny came from a family of Dutch descent in Midland Park, New Jersey, not far from Brooklyn, and a group of five hundred fans, including his parents, had come to see him pitch that night.

Max Butcher, a veteran right-hander, pitched for the Dodgers. In the third inning, Butcher got into trouble. With two men on, Cincinnati first baseman Frank McCormick hit a home run into the left-field stands. The next batter walked and came home on a double. So when Vander Meer came out for the fourth inning, he had a comfortable four-run lead.

Vander Meer warms up for a repeat performance.

In the first six innings no Dodger got as far as second base. Although Vander Meer had walked five batters, he had not given up a single hit. Under the artificial light his fast ball appeared even faster than usual and the Dodgers seemed helpless. No one had imagined that this inexperienced pitcher could repeat his no-hit performance. But by the end of the sixth even faithful Dodger rooters were pulling for Vander Meer. Few baseball fans ever see a no-hit game, but to see a pitcher hurl his second one in a row would be more than extraordinary.

In the seventh inning Vander Meer walked the first two batters. Now the crowd, sensing a Dodger rally, swung back to their home team in sentiment. But Johnny worked his way out of the situation.

He returned to superb form in the eighth inning. He struck out pinch hitter Woody English, retired the next batter on a grounder and struck out the third one.

As Vander Meer walked out to the mound for the ninth inning, Ebbets Field was swept by a tremendous ovation for him. Tension by this time had reached the breaking point. Every pitch was followed by a flutter of excited agitation in the stands.

Vander Meer handled the first out personally. The batter topped a bounder down the first-base side. Johnny fielded it and tagged him out on the first-base line.

Now, with a major league record a few pitches away, the young Cincinnati pitcher appeared to feel the pressure. He walked Babe Phelps, the Dodgers' portly catcher, who then left the game for a pinch runner. Despite his efforts, Vander Meer wasn't able to get his fast ball or his sweeping curve over the plate. The next two batters, Lavagetto and Camilli, walked. Now the bases were loaded with only one out. But the entire crowd, Dodger fans and all, stayed with the left-handed Red this time. Everybody except the Dodgers themselves wanted to see history created.

Center fielder Ernie Koy, an American Indian and a former football star, was the next batter. The right-handed Koy hit a slow roller to third baseman Riggs. It looked like a perfect setup for a double play, but Riggs, playing carefully for the force play at home plate, threw to the catcher so cautiously that there was no time to retire Koy, who was a swift runner, at first base.

Leo Durocher, the Dodger shortstop, was the next batter. He was a weak hitter, but he had a well-known ability to come through under pressure. He hit the first pitch like a rifle shot down the right-field line and the crowd leaped to its feet with a groan. But the drive curved foul into the stands.

The crowd was quiet as Durocher stepped back in to face Vander Meer. This time Johnny gave him

Teammates rush Johnny off the field after his second no-hitter in a row.

a fast ball. Durocher hit an arching fly ball to short center field. Harry Craft, the center fielder, came running and was there to catch it. With the bases loaded, Vander Meer had put the Dodgers away. The score: 6–0.

Great pitchers have come and gone since that night in Brooklyn, but no one has ever pitched two no-hit games in a row. Among those who remember Vander Meer's feat, he is still known as Johnny "Double No-Hit."

25
The Batboy Who Played

The year was 1952. Everywhere the Fitzgerald team of the Georgia State League traveled, Joe Reliford went along. Joe was batboy, clubhouse attendant, equipment boy and general handyboy. He was good-sized for a boy of twelve, almost big enough to be a member of the team. Sometimes the players let him sneak into the batting cage and get a few swings before a game. Joe could swing a bat well.

The players liked Joe because he was good-natured. And Joe liked the players because they were good to him and made him feel like one of them. For a lad in a small southern town, being batboy is a symbol of local stature. Everybody in Fitzgerald, and several other towns in the league, knew Joe Reliford.

Joe's favorite player was the Fitzgerald second baseman, Charlie Ridgeway. Charlie would often sit beside Joe on the bus as they rode through the night on their way home from a game in another town, and he would talk serious baseball with him. This made Joe feel grown up.

Joe liked speed in a baseball player and Ridgeway was the fastest runner in the Georgia State League. One season Ridgeway stole over sixty bases and Joe was certain that he would someday see his hero play in the big leagues. Charlie never made the majors, but before the end of the season, he got a promotion.

One day the president and manager of the Fitz-

171

gerald team, Ace Adams, called Ridgeway into the clubhouse and said, "Charlie, I've got a surprise for you. You're the new manager."

Adams had been managing the team and also trying to handle its business matters. The burden was too much for him, so he appointed Ridgeway his manager on the field.

Ridgeway had been the manager for a week when the Fitzgerald team was scheduled to play the Statesboro team, its rival in the pennant race. The Statesboro Elks Club was sponsoring a special "night" for the home team and a big crowd turned out for the game.

The sight of a filled park seemed to give the Statesboro players a big boost. They bombarded Fitzgerald with base hits, and Joe Reliford looked on sorrowfully as Charlie Ridgeway's new managerial career took a bitter turn. The score became so one-sided that the festive crowd, looking for other means of amusement, began jeering Joe as he trotted out to pick up the bats of Fitzgerald players.

By the eighth inning, Statesboro was leading by the score of 13–0. The fans began shouting the derisive ball-park cry, "Put in the batboy! Put in the batboy!"

By this time, Ridgeway was willing to do anything for relief. "Why not put in the batboy? If the crowd wants a show, we'll give 'em a show," Ridgeway said to himself.

Ridgeway called time and held a quick conference with the umpire, a young man named Eddie Kubick. "They're hollering for the batboy, Eddie," Ridgeway said. "Our batboy's got on a uniform, and he swings a pretty good bat. I've seen him in practice. What's wrong with putting him in the game?"

"Nothing, as far as I know," Kubick said. "But if you win the game, you'll have to forfeit for using an ineligible player."

"The way things are going," Ridgeway said tartly, "that isn't likely to happen. Reliford batting for Nichting."

Ridgeway went back to the dugout and told Joe to get a bat. He told Nichting, the leading hitter on the team, to be seated.

"You're not serious, are you, Mr. Charlie?" Joe asked.

"They've been hollering for a batboy," Ridgeway said, "we'll give 'em the batboy. Get a stick and get up there."

Joe hesitated a moment. Then he grabbed a bat and walked up to the plate. The crowd howled. Curtis White, the Statesboro pitcher, shook his head in disbelief and looked at Kubick. The umpire motioned for the pitch as the announcement was made over the public address system:

"Reliford batting for Nichting."

The crowd howled louder. Joe scratched the dirt with his shoe and waved the bat menacingly. White had a two-hitter going at the time and he was taking no chances. He cut loose with a good fast ball. Joe swung and connected. He smashed the ball toward the third baseman. It looked like a base hit, but the third baseman speared the ball and threw Joe out at first base by a step. Nevertheless, Joe's effort had been valiant, and the crowd now cheered him.

Ridgeway went all the way with his batboy. He threw him Nichting's glove and sent him to right field. One of the Statesboro players, Charlie Quimby, had a hitting streak of twenty-one games going into "Elks Night." While all his teammates had been feasting on Fitzgerald pitching, he was hitless as he came to bat for the last time in the eighth inning. He sent a sinking liner to right field that looked like a certain hit. Joe took out after the ball and just when it looked as though he would never make it, he stuck out his glove and made an acrobatic catch. Ironically Ray Nichting could never have made the catch. Not only was he a slow runner, but he led the league in errors by outfielders that season.

The Statesboro crowd stood and cheered the bat-boy as he ran in from the outfield with a broad grin on his face. Joe never got a chance to go to bat again, because the Fitzgerald team went down in order in the ninth.

It would have been a somber ride back to Fitzgerald that night but for the subject of Joe Reliford. The players, seemingly trying to forget their crushing defeat, carried on loudly and proudly about his part in the game.

"Better sign him to a contract, Skipper," one said to Ridgeway, "before he gets away."

"If he gets any better," said another, "he'll want a bonus."

Ridgeway raised his voice above the noise on the bus and said, "Fellows, if you never make it to the big leagues, you can always say you've done something no big leaguer has ever done. You've played with the youngest professional that ever played baseball."

He put his arm around Joe Reliford and gave him a big wink.

26
The Miracle of Coogan's Bluff

When men around New York City speak of the "Miracle of Coogan's Bluff," they can only be speaking of the year 1951 and the real fairy tale of the New York Giants. There will never be another "Miracle of Coogan's Bluff," because the Giants have moved to San Francisco and their old home park, the Polo Grounds, which was situated at the foot of Coogan's Bluff, has been torn down and replaced by apartment buildings.

The "miracle" belonged to Bobby Thomson, a 27-year-old third baseman and outfielder for the Giants. Thomson was born in Scotland, but his parents came to the United States when he was an infant. He had grown up on Staten Island, just across the bay from the heart of New York City.

He accomplished his feat at the Polo Grounds on October 3, 1951, but the story began almost two months earlier.

On August 11, the Brooklyn Dodgers, the Giants' most bitter rivals, led the National League by a margin of 13½ games. The Giants were in second place. The two teams had only thirty-eight more games to play and catching the Dodgers seemed utterly hopeless—to everyone except the Giants and their manager, Leo Durocher.

The next day, August 12, the Giants went to work on their "miracle." They won sixteen games in a row, cutting the Dodgers' lead to five games. It still seemed unlikely that the Dodgers could be caught. With their fine pitching staff and such sluggers as Gil Hodges and Duke Snider, the Dodgers gave the appearance of great strength. But the Giants had momentum and everything they touched turned to victory.

Finally on Friday, September 28, the Giants caught up with the Dodgers without lifting a bat. While the "miracle men" were idle, Brooklyn lost to Philadelphia, tying themselves with the Giants with two games left. Two days later, the season ended in a tie making a play-off necessary to determine the championship.

The play-off between the Giants and the Dodgers was as exciting as any World Series, and Ebbets Field, home of the Dodgers, was packed for the first game. Jim Hearn of the Giants pitched against Ralph Branca of the Dodgers and Hearn won with a five-hit game, 3–1. Thomson delivered the decisive blow, a two-run homer in the fourth inning. But this was only a warm-up for his "miracle."

In the second game, played at the Polo Grounds, Charlie Dressen, Brooklyn manager, surprised everyone by calling on a rookie pitcher, Clem Labine, just recently brought up from St. Paul, as his starter. Labine turned out to be the perfect choice. He shut out the Giants, 10–0.

In the deciding game, the Dodgers opened with a run in the first inning, taking advantage of veteran Sal Maglie's pitching wildness. In the second inning, something happened that seemed to tell the tense crowd that the Giants were through.

Bobby Thomson came to bat with Whitey Lockman on first base. Since Bobby had touched Branca for the big home run in the first game of the play-off, and since he had been the Giants' biggest hitter during their late-season comeback, excitement ran through the stands.

Thomson delivered. The Giants' third baseman lined a hit into left field. Rounding first base, he sensed that he had a chance to make it to second, and head down, he roared onward. Pulling into second, however, he came face to face with one of the most awful situations of his life. Whom should he meet, already standing safely on the bag, but Whitey Lockman. Lockman had played it safe. With the play on his side of the field he had chosen not to risk taking an extra base. All the Dodgers had to do was tag Thomson, and visions of a big Giant inning vanished.

In the seventh inning the Giants finally got to Newcombe for the tying run. It seemed that fortune was trying to make up to Thomson for the blunder he had pulled in the second inning, for it was he who hit a long fly ball scoring Monte Irvin from third.

Apparent disaster befell the Giants in the eighth inning, however. The Dodgers scored three runs and took a 4–1 lead. Spectators who liked to avoid the end-of-the-game rush began making their way toward the subway. The Giants didn't score in the last of the eighth, nor did the Dodgers in the top of the ninth.

In the last of the ninth, the Giants' Alvin Dark opened with a single off Newcombe. Don Mueller followed with a single that sent Dark to third. Irvin popped up for the first out but Lockman brought new hope to Giant fans by smacking a double that scored Dark and moved Mueller to third. The score was now 4–2, but the Dodgers needed only two more outs for victory.

Dodger Manager Dressen called time and went out to the mound to talk to Newcombe. The big Dodger pitcher stalked about, obviously unsettled and distressed. Failing to calm him down, Dressen motioned to the bullpen in distant left field, and out came Ralph Branca, his black windbreaker thrown over his shoulder. Bobby Thomson was the next batter. Although he had blasted a big home run off Branca two days previously, Dressen felt Branca was the man for the situation.

Thomson stepped into the batter's box, and Branca

delivered. It was a perfectly placed pitch, a fast ball
that slipped over the outside corner of the plate for
a strike.

Branca checked third base, now occupied by Clint

*After a disastrous eighth inning had given the Dodgers a 3-run lead,
Bobby Thomson belted his last-minute homer to win the pennant
play-off, 5–4.*

Bobby danced a jig on his way to home plate and a jubilant welcome.

Hartung, who was running for Mueller, and second base, occupied by Lockman. Then he pitched. The ball came in high, on the inside, out of the strike zone. From his crouched position, however, Thomson took a swing. At first the ball's flight indicated only a long fly to left field, and the left fielder, Andy Pafko, drifted back to take it. But the ball kept traveling and soon Pafko was up against the wall.

As Thomson trotted into first base he turned and took a second look at the ball, then began jumping up and down. The ball had reached the stands—it was a home run!

Hartung scored and Lockman scored, and Thomson followed, dancing a jig down the third base line toward home. By the time he reached the plate, everybody in a Giant uniform, as well as a few over-zealous fans, had come to greet him, and a wildly jubilant celebration took place. With one blow, when all had seemed lost, Bobby Thomson had won the pennant for the Giants in their home at the foot of Coogan's Bluff. His run had made the score 5–4 and the play-off was over. Ralph Branca, who had stood on the pitcher's mound watching the flight of the drive, his body growing limp and his spirit faint, now turned and began the long, lonely walk to the club-house. As he turned, the number on the back of his uniform stood out as if lighted by neon: 13.

INDEX

(Page numbers in italics refer to photographs.)